A BRIEF INTRODUCTION TO

MODERN ARABIC LITERATURE

BRIEF INTRODUCTIONS SERIES

A BRIEF INTRODUCTION TO

MODERN ARABIC LITERATURE

DAVID TRESILIAN

SAQI

London San Francisco Beirut

ISBN: 978-0-86356-405-5

First published by Saqi, 2008

A full CIP record for this book is available from the British Library.

A full CIP record for this book is available from the Library of Congress.

Manufactured in Lebanon

SAQI

26 Westbourne Grove, London W2 5RH
825 Page Street, Suite 203, Berkeley, California 94710
Tabet Building, Mneimneh Street, Hamra, Beirut
www.saqibooks.com

Contents

Illustrations

Acknowledgements

I would like to thank Lawrence Joffe for suggesting this book to me and everyone at Saqi, especially Rebecca O'Connor, for tracking down the pictures and seeing it through the press. The enthusiasm and support of the late Mai Ghoussoub were great sources of encouragement when the book was first discussed. Finally, I am grateful to friends in Paris and Cairo, particularly Asmahan El-Batraoui and Mona Anis, for comments and suggestions that saved me from several false steps.

Introduction

English-speaking readers interested in modern Arabic literature have sometimes not been well served. While more works translated from the Arabic are now available in English than was the case even a few years ago, it is still possible to walk into an ordinary bookstore and find few, if any, works by Arab authors on the shelves. Under such circumstances writing a brief introduction to modern Arabic literature is likely to be a particular challenge. Having been introduced to this literature, how likely is it that readers will be able to explore it for themselves?

Fortunately, the situation is not as bad as it can sometimes seem, and recent years have seen growing interest in literary translation from the Arabic. High-quality translations of the works of many Arab authors are available today, not least those of the winner of the 1988 Nobel Prize for Literature, the late Egyptian novelist Naguib Mahfouz. Even so, in general it still remains the case that Arabic literature is often not well known outside the Arab world, much of the literature produced in the twenty-two countries making up the Arab League, extending, as a phrase used by the Arabs has it, 'from

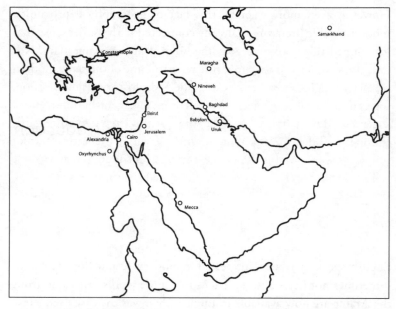

1. Map of the Arab world showing the major literary centres of Cairo, Beirut and Baghdad

the [Atlantic] Ocean to the Gulf, not being translated into European languages and therefore remaining inaccessible except to those able to read Arabic.[1]

This book will argue that this situation is a pity for various reasons. First, there is the obvious loss that it entails for western readers. The Arab world is one of Europe's closest neighbours, and, occupying the whole of the southern and eastern Mediterranean and stretching to the borders of Iran, it is not as far away from us as we might sometimes be encouraged to think. It would be a shame if this region's cultural achievements and debates, as represented in its modern literature, were to remain a closed book to us as a result of translations that are either few in number or that are not widely accessible.

However, even more than by this fact of geographical proximity, modern Arabic literature is already connected with us in a sense that it is hoped this book will go some way towards making plain. Not only does modern Arabic literature refer to some of the same modern history, though seen 'from the other side' – the history of colonization, for example, or of the effects of western involvement in non-western societies – but it has for at least some of the time looked towards European models for inspiration. For those with a theoretical turn of mind, modern Arabic literature provides intriguing material for reflection along lines suggested by fields such as postcolonial studies, translation studies and the emerging study of world literature. Reading it may not only help us to learn about a different set of societies and a different culture from our own, but may also help us to see our own society and culture in a different light.

The aim of this book is first and foremost to suggest some ways in which modern Arabic literature might be thought about, both for the general reader interested to know a little about this literature and for students, not primarily Arabists, engaged in comparative literary study. There are various ways in which the title may be taken. This is a *brief* introduction to modern Arabic literature, and brevity has entailed a considerable degree of compression, though it is hoped that this has not come at the price of too much distortion. Though coverage has had to be sacrificed in order to ensure manageable length, it is hoped that not too much has been left out and not too many authors have gone unmentioned. In terms of scope, for the purposes of this book modern Arabic literature means material written since 1945, the emphasis being placed on recent decades and on prose fiction. However, it is not possible to understand this material without a sense of the historical background, so material written earlier in the century is surveyed, as is – all too briefly – modern Arabic poetry and drama.

Modern Arabic literature, for the purposes of this introduction, also means work originally written in Arabic. This may seem obvious, but so close have relations been between the Arab world and Europe in the modern period that a good deal of Arabic literature has been written in European languages, such as French and English, and a good deal of it is still being written in French. This is particularly the case in those countries situated in the west of the Arab world: Algeria, Morocco and Tunisia, known collectively as the *Maghreb* (which means 'west' in Arabic), all of them previously colonized by France. However, the relationship between the Arabic and French-language material produced in the countries of the Maghreb is controversial, having to do with large issues of culture and identity, and there is a risk of caricature in discussing it in too confined a space. For these reasons, this book deals with literature produced in the east of the Arab world, in Arabic the *Mashraq*, though there are some comments about the Maghreb in Chapter 1 below.[2] This rule has unfortunately also meant the exclusion of Arabic literature written in English and of authors like Ahdaf Soueif and Hisham Matar, as well as of one of the best works of modern Arabic literature to have been written in English, Waguih Ghali's *Beer in the Snooker Club*. The first two writers are widely known; it is a matter for celebration that, four decades after its English publication, Ghali's novel is now available in Arabic translation.[3]

A further point is that while this book aims to discuss literature produced across the Arab world without emphasizing any one 'national' literature, the literary production of modern Egypt is given greater space than that of other countries. There are good reasons for this. Egypt is the largest and oldest of the modern Arab states, and it possesses what has historically been the most influential literary and intellectual milieu. This situation is encapsulated in a phrase sometimes used by the Arabs to the effect that 'Cairo writes, Beirut publishes and Baghdad reads', which reflects a long-standing division of intellectual labour within the Arab world. While this situation

2. Informal bookselling, such as in Cairo, can help overcome perennial problems of distributing books in the Arab world

may be changing, the Iraqi reading public having been decimated by events in that country, and the Beirut publishing industry arguably not having recovered from Lebanon's long civil war, it is still the case that the Cairo literary scene has the longest history and the greatest prestige, even though Egypt may be losing its traditional position of intellectual leadership in the Arab world.[4]

Western writers on Arabic literature, as well as western translators of it, have also traditionally looked to Egypt for materials, with the result that the literary history of Egypt has been worked over more assiduously than that of any other Arab country. It is a fact that most of the literary writing translated from Arabic into European languages is by Egyptian authors.[5] Moreover, Egypt's predominance in the Arab literary scene is reflected in standard works on the subject: in the volume devoted to modern Arabic literature in the *Cambridge History of Arabic Literature*, for example, edited by an Egyptian academic, the lion's share of the space is given over to writing by Egyptian authors.[6] Egyptian intellectuals dominate Arab universities and the Arab media, whether published in Cairo or elsewhere, and the autobiographies of writers and intellectuals from other Arab countries often talk of their authors having had an Egyptian teacher of Arabic at school, or of growing up reading Egyptian literature, watching Egyptian films or listening to Egyptian music.

For the Algerian writer Yasmina Khadra, for example, while 'learning to write' meant 'learning to write in French', where writing in Arabic is concerned the giants consist of Egyptian authors familiar across the Arab world, such as 'Tewfik El Hakim ... Youcef As-Soubai, Hafed Ibrahim, Najib Mahfoud' and Taha Hussein.[7] Similarly, when growing up in Morocco in the 1950s the young Mohamed Berrada, later a well-known novelist and critic, dreamt of going to Cairo, the centre of Arab national aspirations and Arabic literature and culture at the time. When he finally had the opportunity to leave Morocco as a student, he chose Cairo above Damascus because 'his head was filled with scenes from [Egyptian] films such as *Vive l'amour*, *Love is Forbidden* and *Passion and Vengeance*, with the songs of Mohamed Abdel-Wahhab, Farid el-Atrache, Asmahan and Umm Kulthoum, and with the names of writers like Taha Hussein, Tawfiq al-Hakim, Manfalouti and Ahmed Lutfi el-Sayyed.'[8] Over more recent decades Egyptians have provided much of the intellectual manpower for Saudi Arabia and the Gulf countries: Egypt's brain-drain, long a feature of that country, has in recent decades tended to go eastwards rather than westwards as a result of the superior economic resources of the latter-named countries.

This book reflects the importance of Egypt's writers in modern Arabic literature, while also trying to give other countries their due. This is particularly the case in the discussion of modern Arabic poetry, where other Arab writers have arguably been more important than Egyptian. It is the case, too, in the extended treatment given to modern Palestinian literature in Chapter 4. Marked by dispossession, diaspora and ongoing occupation, modern Palestine has given rise to a literature that is in certain respects unique in the Arab world, and Palestinian writers and intellectuals have enjoyed an influence in Arab letters out of all proportion to the country's size, matching the role that Palestine and the Israeli-Palestinian conflict has played in Arab affairs since the end of the Second World War.

That being said, while for some purposes it is useful, or even essential, to emphasize a writer's local affiliations, seen in a larger perspective those affiliations may not tell the whole story. Mahfouz, for example, while a very 'Egyptian' writer who wrote throughout his life about his native city of Cairo, is also an author who has an audience across the Arab world, and any literate Arab is likely to have read his works (or to have seen the films made from them). Indeed, owing to its use of a common language and its references to shared cultural and historical experiences, Arabic literature, like the Arab world, can be viewed in a double perspective, being at once all of a piece and divided

15

up into local, 'national' parts. Arab writers tend to address both their immediate countrymen and the wider readership provided by the Arab world, and for this reason, it makes sense to speak of Mahfouz as being as much an 'Arab writer' as he is a local, 'Egyptian' one.

Finally, modern Arabic literature, like other literatures, can be read with various aims in mind. One of the main reasons, traditionally, has been linguistic, as part of the learning of Arabic; though because of the way in which Arabic studies have sometimes been organized one may get the impression that students of Arabic, who are among the people most qualified to enjoy the modern literature, may actually be among those least likely to do so. All too often, enjoyment has been drummed out of them by a long process of linguistic initiation. The kind of memories that sometimes remain from the learning of Latin at school, or of struggling through Anglo-Saxon and the Middle English dialects as part of an English degree, sometimes also linger from learning Arabic. Sometimes such memories remain even for the Arabs themselves, for special reasons mentioned in Chapter 1. One hastens to add that this book mostly discusses works that are available in English translation, and no knowledge of Arabic is required.

Another reason for reading modern Arabic literature is sociological, the literature serving as a source of information on the societies that produced it. It is natural to read literary material in this way, and the ways in which such material is discussed at school or university on the whole tends to reinforce it. Students everywhere are perhaps familiar with the kind of essay that asks them to consider what might be learned from a work of literature about attitudes to gender, or class, or ethnicity in the society that produced it. Modern Arabic literature, too, can be read in this way, and indeed this book to an extent does so.

However, it is as well to strike a note of caution at the outset. While modern Arabic literature can of course be read sociologically, this approach naturally does not exhaust its interest. Indeed, one of the prime purposes of this brief introduction is to show that modern Arabic literature can be read for pleasure and enjoyment, like any other kind of literary writing (with allowance made for the fact that it is read in translation). One does not only go to it in search of material for academic study or for information that can then be used for other purposes. Indeed, there are reasons why this attitude has in the past been met with by suspicion, again for reasons mentioned in Chapter 1. Like all imaginative literature, modern Arabic literature is perhaps best read for its own sake, as part of a process of imaginative expansion that culminates in enhanced understanding.

Clearly, the choices that translators and publishers of modern Arabic literature make when presenting it to western readers also determine the picture that those readers form of it, and the sometimes controversial issues of translation and cultural exchange are discussed in more detail below. In concluding this section, however, it may be as well to say something about the *variety* of modern Arabic literature, something which is not always evident to western readers. Arabic literary writing can serve as a vehicle for reflection on questions of history, identity and individual life-options. But it also contains works that interpret the role of literature differently, pushing it towards linguistic or formal experiment rather than towards realism, or that see literature as a vehicle for the expression of minority identity or sexual difference. While some Arab writers have an official status within their countries of origin and are familiar faces on international conference circuits, others are oppositional figures. While some authors, like many authors everywhere, seek to reach the widest possible audience, others are writers' writers and write primarily for their peers.

Few, if any, Arab authors manage to make a living from their writings alone, and probably there are none that reach the kind of audiences that a writer of a western bestseller can expect to reach. There is no

Arab J. K. Rowling, and some western critics have even accused Arab writers of being insufficiently commercially minded.[9] Almost none of them benefit from the kind of promotion routinely available to successful writers in the West, and on the whole the Arab publishing industry does not have access to the impressive production, distribution and promotion techniques available to its western peers. While there are now more pan-Arab publishing ventures than there once were, thanks to the improved distribution made possible by the Internet, and there are substantially more literary prizes, some of them highly lucrative, in general terms the publishing industry in Arab countries is still under-developed, and this has negative impacts on authors' careers. Despite the high esteem in which literature is generally held in the Arab world, it often finds few readers.[10]

Some of these sociological issues are touched upon in what follows in the discussion of individual works and authors. A final note concerns spelling conventions and references. For ease of reference in this book the names of Arab authors have been given according to their published English versions (e.g. Naguib Mahfouz). A book in itself could be written on Arabic personal names, which are constructed more along the Russian lines of given name, patronymic name, and family name than on the first name-family name pattern familiar in the West. The situation is complicated by the fact that by no means every Arab will use a family name, called a *nasab* or *laqab*, constructing a three-part name instead that consists of a given name followed by the father's and grandfather's given names. No Arab writer would refer to the Egyptian intellectual Taha Hussein as 'Hussein', for example, as this book does, since Hussein is the author's father's name. As in the case of spellings, however, western conventions are followed in this book for ease of reference. On the few occasions where Arabic words or phrases are given in the text these are spelled more or less as they sound. Translations from French are by the author. Translations from Arabic are from published English translations, sometimes slightly modified. To avoid cluttering the text, references have been kept as brief as possible. While space has been saved by omitting many page references, the sources of all quotations have been given.

Reading Arabic Literature

Orientalism, a well-known work by the late Palestinian-American critic Edward Said, develops the thought that a particular way of seeing has historically vitiated relations between the Arab world and Europe. This way of seeing, dubbed 'orientalism', has been present in various European representations of the Arab world and the Arabs, whether literary, artistic, academic or in the media, and these have circulated widely in western societies, European representations giving way to North American ones. 'Orientalism', Said writes, is 'a way of coming to terms with the Orient that is based on the Orient's special place in European Western experience', that 'special place' being as Europe's 'other', everything Europe is not. Whereas Europeans have sometimes considered themselves to be 'rational, virtuous, mature, [and] "normal"', among other things, the Orient has been seen as 'irrational, depraved (fallen), childlike, [and] "different"', particularly in the period after 1800 and in the 'discourse' of orientalism.[1]

While Said's book has been controversial and continues to generate debate,[2] its contribution lies in drawing attention to the ways in which the Arab world has been represented in Europe and the purposes such representations have served. It drew attention, for example, to a class of intellectual middlemen, the writers, painters, photographers, professors and officials whose views the book examined in detail, as well as to the less-celebrated work of journalists and translators, who file reports on the Arab world or translate materials from one set of societies into forms that can be understood by another. The work of all these people has helped to determine the picture that Europeans and perhaps westerners more generally have been able to form of the Arab world and of Arab history and culture. 'Everyone who writes about the Orient must locate himself *vis-à-vis* the Orient,' wrote Said, 'which add[s] up to deliberate ways of addressing the reader, containing the Orient, and finally, representing it or speaking in its behalf.'

While it would be too much to suggest that there is any 'correct' way of seeing the Arab world, either in absolute terms or in terms uninfected by the considerations pointed to by Said, it may be possible to arrive at a more informed picture than the one criticized in *Orientalism*. That, at least, is the aim of this book, which seeks neither to 'represent' the Orient nor to 'speak in its behalf' but rather to survey works by men and women who have contributed to modern Arabic literature, and, it is hoped, to allow them to speak through their works available in translation. Nevertheless, Said's work can be helpful in suggesting ways into reading modern Arabic literature, as well as in thinking about ways in which it has sometimes been read. These concern the manner in which this literature has been approached by western readers, in other words the issues of reception and translation pointed to in *Orientalism*; the features of it that present particular challenges to non-Arabic-speaking readers, such as unfamiliar cultural references and the special character of the Arabic language; and the geographical spread of the Arab world and its own internal divisions that should be borne in mind when approaching its literature.

These themes naturally lead to consideration of the conditions under which modern Arabic literature circulates in its countries of origin, as well as to examination of it as a form of 'postcolonial' or 'world' literature, when seen from Europe, and reflection on its present situation. Having begun early in the last century as a new form of expression, based – at least for works in prose and drama – in some measure on European models, it has now become a flourishing component of Arab societies.

Translators of modern Arabic literature have sometimes stressed how difficult it is for works by modern Arab writers to sell in western countries. Denys Johnson-Davies, for example, probably the best-known translator of modern Arabic literature into English, has pointed to the demands that determine which texts get translated and the ways in which they are marketed and, presumably, to some extent read. There is no point in doing a translation that will not be published, but many translations have nevertheless ended up in the drawers of translators' desks because they have failed to find western publishers. And there are also other issues. Literary translators from Arabic into English have sometimes possessed what Johnson-Davies describes as 'excessive power', since they play a 'pioneering role in uncovering and furthering writing' they believe to be valuable, with English or other foreign publishers not necessarily being well informed about the Arab literary scene.[3] They have also had to respond to pressures in the target market, notably for works that answer either to a particular conception of what Arab societies are like, whether 'picturesque' or 'repressive', or to existing western interests, with regard to women's experience, for example, or the experience of minorities. Basic to a translator's choice of works to translate is whether or not these will find a publisher, and this tends to mean that translators choose material they consider will sell in western countries, a commercial choice, or material that answers to their conception of literary 'talent', an aesthetic or even a political one.

The ways in which such choices determine the translation of non-western literatures and the images of such literatures formed by western readers as a result have been investigated in recent years. It is well known, for example, that the 'boom' in Latin American writing that swept western publishing in the 1960s and 1970s, propelling a previously little-known body of work to international fame, took place in part because that writing answered to the needs of the western marketplace. It sold. According to one assessment, by the early 1970s North American and European readers 'knew what they wanted from Latin America: magical realism ... the genre which presented the region's realities in hyperbolic surrealist terms, the genre which portrayed the exoticizing image of Latin America that readers found intriguing and entertaining, [and the genre that represented] a wild regressive liberating escape from the humdrum of ordinary progressive overly civilized life.'[4] This added up to an image of Latin American writing among European and North American readers that was not necessarily one that readers from one of the many countries involved may have had of their own society's literary production. But it was an image that was self-perpetuating as far as western readers were concerned, since it dictated the works that publishers were likely to consider for publication and the choices made by those translating them.

While sales considerations dictate commercial choices, there are also aesthetic considerations underlying them. Readers of translated works of foreign literature tend to respond best to works that fit in with their pre-existing tastes and interests. While it is not impossible for a work that lies outside these to be successfully translated, marketed and sold, in this way creating the taste by which it is to be read, in general the closer a work lies to the expectations and interests of foreign readers the more likely it is to be translated and the greater the success it is likely to enjoy in the target market, whatever that work's status may be in its country of origin. 'Magical realism' answered notably well to a demand in western societies for a particular image of Latin America and for a type of literature that seemed to convey it. As a result, for a time Latin American literature *was* magical realism, even if, in fact, there were other competing styles.

While literary writing in Arabic did not benefit from the boom conditions that put Latin American literature on the map in the 1960s and 1970s, the processes underlying the translation of modern Arabic literature into European languages can be understood in similar terms. Until the award of the Nobel Prize for Literature to the Egyptian novelist Naguib Mahfouz in 1988, for example, modern Arabic literature was perhaps a literature of only marginal international interest, something indicated not only by the statistics for published literary translations from the Arabic, but also by the choice of works translated and the way in which these were promoted.

Salih Altoma, for example, notes that between 1947 and 1967, only sixteen modern literary titles were translated from Arabic into English, this picking up to a further eighty-four between 1967 and 1988, possibly as a result of political tensions in the Middle East and certainly thanks to the efforts of a handful of translators and a few dedicated publishers. After 1988, however, this trickle became a flood.[5] Early translations tended to be of works that could either be easily assimilated to western interests or that portrayed the West in a flattering light. They gave little sense of the literary landscape as a whole, or the place of the translated writers within it, as is perhaps indicated by the failure of repeated attempts to secure the Nobel Prize for Literature for Taha Hussein, one of the most important of all Arab writers, before the latter's death in 1973. It is a sobering thought that even as late as the 1990s, according to a recent biographer, one of the best-known Arab authors among western readers was Gibran Kahlil Gibran, an expatriate Lebanese whose writings served a taste for the exotic and the 'spiritual' in a manner drawing on late nineteenth-century symbolism. 'He came from the East,' his biographer writes, 'which was beginning to be equated with a more spiritual approach to life.'[6] But Gibran's meaning in the Arab context is quite different from that he was given, or played up to, among his western readers. Whereas in the Arab world Gibran is seen as a historically significant, though still minor, figure in the development of modern Arabic poetry, among western readers he has sometimes been taken at his own estimation as a kind of 'prophetic' writer, one who articulates supposedly eternal themes.[7]

Works of modern Arabic literature that were translated up to as late as the 1970s commonly either served documentary purposes, giving information on 'manners and customs' in the manner of European travel literature though with greater claims to authenticity, or answered to particular western agendas, such as the desire to see the Arab world as 'backward', enlightenment coming to it as a result of the impact of the West, or Arab women, in particular, as repressed, achieving freedom through their adoption of what were seen as western ideas of female emancipation. The French writer Richard Jacquemond, for example, comments that Taha Hussein's autobiography, *The Days*, and Tawfiq al-Hakim's novel *Diary of a Country Prosecutor* (discussed in Chapter 2), were translated into French in the 1930s, probably in part because both works draw a contrast between a 'backward' native society and the impact of enlightened European ideas. This contrast is also apparent in translated works by Arab women, both then and now, those that are the most often translated drawing a contrast 'between the liberating values associated with the West that their authors defend and the sexual oppression of the 'oriental male' that they denounce.'[8] This has led to decades of controversy over the translation and promotion in the West of works by Arab women, from those of Out el-Koloub (written in French), criticized in the 1930s by Taha Hussein, to those of Nawal al-Saadawi, Alifa Rifaat and others, discussed in Chapter 6.

Following Mahfouz's award of the Nobel Prize, however, the translation of modern Arabic literature received a tremendous fillip, though this success was not without ironies of its own. Arabic literature was still expected to conform to a particular western image of it, and anything not doing so found a foreign market only with difficulty, or not at all. While Mahfouz was remarkable for having reinvented himself more than once over the course of a long career, many of his most accomplished novels, dating from the 1950s, are written according to the familiar canons of nineteenth-century realism. This means that much of his best work is not representative of the work of Arab writers from the 1970s to the present day. Yet, such features of Mahfouz's career, and of the post-war development of modern Arabic literature more generally, were flattened out in the reception of the novels in the West. For many western readers, modern Arabic literature was understood to be simply rather like the earlier works of Naguib Mahfouz. Moreover, while Mahfouz is often read in the Arab world as an experimental, or even subversive writer, in western societies he has tended to be seen as a kind of latter-day Dickens, accomplished certainly, and containing lots of local 'colour', but easily assimilated as a kind of fluent foreign pupil of established European styles. Jacquemond, for example, comments that Mahfouz has commonly been received abroad as the 'ethnographer of the "ordinary people of Cairo", who have been frozen into the "brightly coloured" image that their "chronicler" has produced of them, like figures in an orientalist painting.'⁹ Nothing could be further from the truth.

Taken together, these factors have tended to produce an image of modern Arab literature that is both old-fashioned and picturesque, even Mahfouz's success with international readers having produced an idea of the literature as a whole that is in many respects misleading. Who would have guessed from the reception of Mahfouz's earlier novels that their author was also the author of experimental, 'modernist' thrillers? Or that the earlier novels are politically engaged? Or, indeed, that modern Arabic literature, at least from the 1960s on, has in large part consisted of writing that is quite unlike the earlier or later works of Mahfouz? (It has, of course, been even more unlike the works of Gibran.) Fortunately, the greater availability of translations today, and the greater transparency of the Arab world in the post-cold war period, has meant that many, though by no means all, of these preconceptions are disappearing.

Such issues have to do with the expectations that western readers may bring to literary texts translated from the Arabic and the kinds of text that may be offered to them. They also have to do with the limited options available to Arab writers wishing to build an international career and the few niches available to them in the international marketplace. Yet there are also other, perhaps more technical, issues to bear in mind when reading Arabic literature in translation, as in reading any translation, and these include the ways in which unfamiliar cultural and other references in the 'source' text are rendered in the 'target language' of the translation. How much is it necessary to know about the societies from which they come in order to enjoy these foreign texts? Such issues are complicated in the case of translation from Arabic by the diversity of the Arab world and by specific features of the Arabic language.

There was a time when it was standard practice when translating literature from Arabic into English to do so in an antiquated style, as if the intention was to cast an air of mystery or exoticism over the text. Nineteenth-century translations of classical works of Arabic literature, such as Burton's version of *The Arabian Nights*, are famous for this style, 'a sort of composite mock-Gothic, combining elements from Middle English, the Authorised Version of the Bible and Jacobean drama,' in the words of one commentator,[10] though in an era when 'modern' poetry could still be written in the medieval idiom of Tennyson it was perhaps considered natural to render foreign material in the language of Fitzgerald's *Rubaiyat of Omar Khayyam* (supposedly a 'translation' from Persian).[11] However, 'antiquing' of this sort has sometimes also been considered appropriate even for works of modern Arabic literature, with the result that characters speaking the modern language have been given a spurious 'medieval' or 'exotic' feel. Perhaps this is what Said had in mind when he criticized a tendency among European writers to supply 'orientals with a [picturesque] mentality, a genealogy, an atmosphere' that placed them firmly in the past. Early twentieth-century Arab poets come out sounding like minor nineteenth-century romantics or eighteenth-century clergymen, for example, in A. J. Arberry's versions of them, still among the few available.[12] Moreover, in the case of translating Arabic general problems of translation are heightened by the existence of a 'gap' between the languages that is as much cultural as linguistic. It is unfortunately true that an informed reading of Arabic literature calls for some knowledge of Arab culture and societies. Fortunately, however, this knowledge can be acquired precisely through reading works of literature.

The first chapter of the English translation of Mahfouz's novel *Palace Walk*, the first of the novels making up the *Cairo Trilogy*, for example, includes the following paragraph reproducing the thoughts of Amina, wife of Ahmad Abd al-Jawad, who is a member of Cairo's early twentieth-century middle class:

> She had been terrified of the night when she had first lived in this house. She knew far more about the world of the jinn than that of mankind and remained convinced that she was not alone in the big house. There were demons who could not be lured away from these spacious, empty old rooms for long. Perhaps they had sought refuge there before she herself had been brought to the

house, even before she saw the light of day. She frequently heard their whispers. Time and again she was awakened by their warm breath. When she was left alone, her only defence was reciting the opening prayer of the Qur'an and sura one hundred and twelve from it, about the absolute supremacy of God, or rushing to the lattice-work screen at the window to peer anxiously through it at the lights of the carts and the coffeehouses, listening carefully for a laugh or a cough to help her regain her composure.[13]

In their translation, the translators suggest both the particular situation of Amina, who comes from a traditional family and whose husband has confined her to the house, and the general costs that traditional life entails for women like her in terms of their isolation and segregation from the world outside. Amina is illiterate, and the modernization that was to be such a feature of twentieth-century Arab societies has not yet reached the Cairo middle classes, particularly not the female members of them. Taken as a whole, the *Cairo Trilogy* can be understood as a kind of 'grand narrative' that shows the passing of traditionalist conceptions of life, as well as of much of the patriarchal authority that sustained them.

These considerations are certainly present in the original text, and the translators have preserved features of it like the *jinn* and the *suras* from the *Qur'an* without resorting to footnotes or paraphrased explanation. While the *jinn* may be familiar to western readers as the often malevolent beings described as 'genies' in translations of *The Arabian Nights*, the *suras*, or chapters, of the *Qur'an* may be less so. *Sura* 112, for example, which consists of just four lines of text, is usually called 'The Unity' in English, since it deals with the oneness of God, while the opening prayer of the *Qur'an* is termed the *Fatiha*, which means the 'opening', or introduction, to the whole. Any translator of Arabic literature needs to strike a balance between references that western readers may reasonably be expected to know (such as to the *jinn*), those that they can infer (that a *sura* is a chapter of the *Qur'an*), and those that they may not know but that are not strictly necessary to appreciate the text. The 'lattice-work screen' that Amina peers through onto the street below is *mashrabiyya*, for example, a form of decorative turned wood that made it possible for women to see out of their houses without being seen in them. It will be familiar to anyone who knows the traditional areas of Cairo and other Arab cities.

While the translators have made this novel available to English-speaking readers in such a way that the world it presents is neither unjustly naturalized nor exoticized, Arabic writing sometimes presents more difficult problems, as in the case of the Sudanese novelist Tayeb Salih's 1966 novel *Season of Migration to the North*, one of the most important written in Arabic in that turbulent decade. A paragraph from Denys Johnson-Davies's translation reads:

> 'You're not only drunk but mad,' said Mahjoub. 'Mustafa Sa'eed is in fact the Prophet El-Khidr, suddenly making his appearance and as suddenly vanishing. The treasures that lie in this room are like those of King Solomon, brought here by genies, and you have the key to that treasure. Open, Sesame, and let's distribute the gold and jewels to the people.' Mahjoub was about to shout out and gather the people together had I not put my hand over his mouth. The next morning each of us woke up in his own house not knowing how he'd got there.[14]

There is no explanatory material included with the translation, presumably because the translator wants it to stand on its own without support. Nevertheless, in this case the decision to present the text 'as it is' may have come at the price of full comprehension on the reader's part. *Season of Migration* recounts the stories of an anonymous narrator and an enigmatic older man, Mustafa Sa'eed, both of whom have returned to village life in the Sudan following extended periods abroad, during which they were studying for higher degrees. Whereas the narrator at first believes that this experience has not changed him, and that he is as much at home in the village on his return as he was when he left, Mustafa Sa'eed appears to have had greater difficulty in integrating the two sides of his personality, that part of him that is Sudanese and that part of him acquired through education abroad in a foreign culture. At the point in the text from which this paragraph comes, Mustafa Sa'eed and the contents of his house are being discussed, Sa'eed being compared to the Prophet El-Khidr, a legendary figure who first appeared in the *Qur'an* and subsequently played a prominent part in various popular stories,[15] and the contents of his house to the fabled treasure of the Biblical King Solomon, who, according to the version presented in the *Qur'an*, had power over the *jinn*.[16] The story of the treasure of course comes from the story of 'Ali Baba and the Forty Thieves' in *The Arabian Nights*, Ali Baba's command 'Open Sesame' being familiar to generations of English pantomime-goers. In Arabic the command is 'iftah ya sim sim', meaning the same thing.[17] The scene incidentally appeared for many years on the wall of one of the Cairo cafés in which Naguib Mahfouz used to hold his literary meetings.

Some of this material might come to the minds of western readers reaching this passage, as it might do to Arab readers, but it is unlikely that all of it will. While *Season of Migration*, a novel that has its own fascinating rhythm, can probably manage to hurry the reader past such local difficulties without explanation on the translator's part, this may not be the case for other novels and other novelists, perhaps particularly not for more recent works that have employed pre-modern Arab literary materials, or have used cultural references obscure even to speakers of Arabic. Here the problem is that readers are likely simply to get bored by texts they cannot understand, and such problems are only exacerbated in the case of modern Arabic poetry, much of which employs a quite different rhetoric, and addresses the reader in a quite different way, from, say, most contemporary English poetry. A novel like the *Kitab al-tajalliyat* by the contemporary Egyptian novelist Gamal al-Ghitany, for example, may well be almost unintelligible to western readers without a battery of footnotes, as its French translator has admitted, and even then there is the larger problem of appreciating the writer's interest in his way of proceeding.[18]

In addition to such problems of translation and presentation, there is also a particular problem that the Arabic language presents for any translator, and this perhaps goes some way towards explaining what can sometimes come across as the rather 'stilted' quality of even some of the best literary translations from Arabic. This problem is related to the *diglossia* of the Arabic language, in other words to the fact that the written and the spoken languages are very different from each other. Because of the way in which Arabic has developed, the written language has remained constant over time, with the result that, allowing for some changes in vocabulary and the simplification of style, the language of the *Qur'an*, a text first set down in the seventh century CE, is close to that of modern books and newspapers. This means that an educated Arab reader can read both materials with something like the same degree of facility. It goes without saying that such a situation is impossible to imagine for a language such as English, which achieved its modern form comparatively late and for which the equivalent seventh-century form might be the Anglo-Saxon used in *Beowulf*. Yet, while written Arabic has remained remarkably constant, and is constant from one end of the Arab world to the other, the spoken language has changed over time, and there is often a great distance in matters of vocabulary and grammatical structure between the spoken and written languages. The dialects of Arabic spoken in different parts of the Arab world are sometimes almost mutually unintelligible. Furthermore, the written and the spoken languages have different connotations: while the written language bespeaks a high level of education, the spoken language has people's experience behind it. It is hard to imagine anyone telling a joke in 'classical' Arabic or even having a day-to-day conversation in it, which is why it is often fascinating to watch Arab television and note the speakers' linguistic choices.

This situation complicates literary expression in various ways. In the first place, there is the question of the appropriate language to use in literary texts. While no one supposes that people in real life express themselves quite in the way that characters do in novels, the historical development of the realist novel in Europe has nevertheless gone hand in hand with a desire to use the 'actual language' in literary texts, rather than the 'artificial' language associated with literature. This means that there has tended to be little or no stylistic distinction between direct or indirect speech in novels, making possible realist styles like free indirect discourse, in which the voice of the narrator mixes with the thoughts of the characters, or modernist styles such as stream of consciousness or internal monologue, in which the language of the narration is presumed to coincide with the actual thoughts of the characters.

These styles are of course possible in Arabic narrative, and Mahfouz, for example, has used all of them, free indirect discourse in the *Trilogy*, and stream of consciousness and internal monologue in the shorter novels written in the 1960s. Yet, an Arab writer still has choices to make that can be avoided in English. Should the characters speak using the colloquial language they would actually use, for example, or should the novelist 'translate' their speech and thoughts up a peg or two in the interests of decorum? If the novelist does this, as convention demands, then the result can be a flattening out of the voices present in the novel. If the novelist does not do it, and uses the colloquial language instead, then readers not familiar with the dialect may not be able to understand what the characters are saying. There is the additional problem of how the 'vernacular' or 'colloquial' language, which almost by definition does not exist in written form, can properly be represented in writing. How should one spell it, for example? Moreover, an Arab writer choosing to write in the dialect might also be accused of offences ranging from undermining pan-Arab unity, since readers in one part of the Arab world will not be able to understand the writings of another if the dialect is used, to encouraging sloppy linguistic habits, since the vernacular obviously does not depend, unlike the standard language, on formal education.

While an author's choice of language is a fascinating subject in its own right, for the purposes of this book linguistic issues have only been referred to when they have some special importance. Mahfouz, for example, always used the written language, never the colloquial, and this choice seems to have had something to do with his conception of Arabic literature and the cultural mission of the writer as offering a model of correctness to his readers. This role was common to the writers of the *nahda*, or Arab renaissance, discussed in Chapter 2, who saw themselves as modernizing and reinvigorating the Arabic language as well as Arabic literature.[19] Mahfouz's fellow Egyptian writer Tawfiq al-Hakim, on the other hand, was prepared to entertain the use of the colloquial, particularly since his preferred form of expression was drama: many people have thought there is something ridiculous in having characters from various walks of life all express themselves in formal speech. Al-Hakim's solution was something he called the 'third language', a sort of 'educated speech' that could be read as either standard language or vernacular depending on the desire of the reader.[20]

An author's use of language can say something about his or her conception of literature and the audience he or she wishes to reach. While the use of the vernacular is not necessarily a wholly anti-elitist gesture, since the truly marginalized can neither read nor write, nodding in its direction can nevertheless function as an attack on literary hierarchies of 'high' or 'low' or on the division between the culture of the establishment and the culture of the masses. This is the case, for example, in its occasional use in stories by the Egyptian writer Youssef Idris, discussed in Chapter 3, or in the work of his compatriot Yahya al-Taher Abdullah. It can also serve as a way of asserting regional or national specificity. The novels of Tayeb Salih are full of the language of the Sudan, for example, though the grammar used is standard. The Libyan writer Ibrahim al-Koni and the Egyptian Nubian Haggag Oddoul, discussed in Chapter 6, have also made vernacular language a badge of regional identity against the standard language's powerfully centralizing pull.

A last issue to bear in mind when reading modern Arabic literature is the geographical spread of the Arab world and its division into the countries of the *Mashraq,* situated in the eastern Mediterranean and south-west Asia, and those of the *Maghreb,* situated in North Africa. The standard formula describing literary production in the Arab world, 'Cairo writes, Beirut publishes and Iraq reads', is clearly only good for the Mashraq; in the Maghreb, Algiers has also 'written', as has Tunis or Casablanca, producing an Arabic literature in French following the independence of the countries of the Maghreb from France in the 1950s or early 60s. Algerian authors of the stature of Kateb Yacine, Mohamed Dib and Assia Djebar are not considered in this book, nor are Moroccans like Tahar Ben Jelloun, since they wrote, or write, in French, not Arabic. They are, however, all distinguished contributors to modern Arabic literature. Nevertheless, lines have to be drawn somewhere. Perhaps the modern literature of the Maghreb will be the subject of another book in this series. Naturally, there is also an Arabic literature written in Arabic in the countries of the Maghreb, leading figures including Tahir Wattar, whose novel *The Earthquake* is available in English, Waciny Laredj and Mohamed Choukri, who is one of the best-known Arab novelists internationally thanks to his novel *For Bread Alone*, introduced to western audiences by the American writer Paul Bowles (the French translation, intriguingly different from the English, is by Tahar Ben Jelloun).[21] Nevertheless, this literature, too, must be considered as separate from the focus of this book, which is on the east of the Arab world.

Two last points might be borne in mind when reading modern Arabic literature from a position outside the Arab world. The first of these has to do with Arab publishing, readership and, broadly speaking, the role that literature plays in Arab societies. The second concerns some contemporary western academic approaches to literature that may be relevant to reading modern Arabic literature.

Unlike in western societies, where industry consolidation has become the norm, Arab publishing tends to be arranged more like British publishing before the Second World War, with many small houses producing specialized lists, some of them only numbering a handful of titles a year and these having limited distribution. Some of the most important Cairo publishers in literature and the humanities, for example, are small concerns, often run by their founders, though there are also some larger private-sector publishers and a handful of public-sector publishers in Cairo, a legacy of the Nasser-era nationalizations. This pattern of an assortment of small private-sector publishers, often no more than extensions of bookstores or private ventures by individuals, combined with a few larger private-sector concerns and an overbearing state sector is reproduced in many Arab countries.[22]

In the formula quoted above, Cairo is imagined as originating literary works that are then printed and distributed in Beirut and read in Iraq. However, this has become less true, chiefly because the reasons that once made Beirut an attractive centre for publishers – the comparative freedom of the Lebanese capital when compared with the rest of the Arab world and its links to wider markets – now also obtain in other Arab capitals. Following the US-led invasion of Iraq in 2003, and the years of UN sanctions against the country before it, there is now no publishing industry in Iraq and few possibilities for the population to obtain books. However, western capitals, among them London, have emerged as centres of Arab publishing, and it is not uncommon to find works of modern literature that would perhaps in previous years have been published in Beirut now published either in Beirut and in London, or in London alone. The development of the Internet has also led to changes in Arab publishing. While the distribution of books in Arabic is still extraordinarily poor, books published in one Arab country often being unavailable in another, the advent of the Internet has meant that readers who have access to a computer and a bank account can in theory order books from a Beirut- or London-based online bookseller. Even so, for most people the only occasion on which anything like the full range of Arab publishing is open to display or purchase is during one of the Arab world's many book fairs, like the one that takes place in Cairo every January. A European event is the Salon Euro-Arabe du Livre, held biannually at the Institut du Monde Arabe in Paris.

Such considerations have meant that while it is usually not difficult for Arab authors to be published – quite a few publish their books themselves – it is much more difficult to gain a public profile or readership, and it is almost impossible to make a living from writing books. As a result, Arab authors almost always have full-time jobs, often in the large bureaucracies that are a feature of Arab countries, reserving their writing for their spare time. It is well known, for example, that Mahfouz kept a steady job almost up to the end of his life, first as a bureaucrat and then as a newspaper commentator, and many memoirs by Arab writers complain about both the need to earn a living and the absence of public interest in their literary work. The temptation is always strong to take some bureaucratic job, which can have disastrous effects on an author's writing.

Today, however, these things may be changing, the traditionally

3. The Cairo International Book Fair, held every January, attracts thousands of visitors who buy books published across the Arab world

penniless Arab literary world having received cheering injections of money from the oil-rich Gulf countries. Sometimes lucrative pan-Arab literary awards have replaced fading state patronage in countries such as Egypt, and regional outlets in the shape of the dozens of magazines and newspapers now put out in the Gulf countries can also provide Arab authors with ready cash and even careers, and their appearance has given rise to publishing strategies that would have seemed quite foreign to an 'old-fashioned' author like Mahfouz. While in the past Arab authors published where they could, for example in Beirut to escape harsher conditions at home, today a more usual strategy might be to approach the problem of making a living from books almost in the manner of a European author, serializing a novel in a newspaper in one country, publishing a short story in a magazine in another, and then bringing out the novel or the short stories in book form, which in most cases will make the author far less money. Such strategies have the advantage that an author can reach multiple audiences through them, and it is always possible that the readers of newspapers or magazines may be tempted to purchase the later book, if they can get hold of it.

Nevertheless, while Arab authors now have a greater range of outlets for their work and at least in theory better distribution of it, it still remains the case that Arab writers are poorly professionalized. Publishing contracts are non-standard or non-existent, copyright protection is poor, and books sell in very small numbers given the size of the potential readership. There are few literary agents in the Arab world, and censorship remains a problem in many Arab countries. Furthermore, the present climate of religious conservatism in the Arab world has meant that some 'secular' authors have either fallen silent or have gone into exile following threats against them, or they have seen their work banned following press and religious campaigns against it. Under such circumstances, some writers have sought to develop a reputation abroad and in translation instead, though this strategy too is not without its costs.[23]

Arabic literature does not exist in isolation, and it can also be looked at comparatively as a variety of 'postcolonial' literature, though still a relatively unfamiliar one, as well as a case study in the arena of 'world literature'.

Postcolonial studies are perhaps more indebted to Arabic literature than their later inflections might suggest, since one of the foundational texts of this academic discipline, Said's *Orientalism*, dealt precisely with representations of the Arab world in Europe and the West. Questions of representation and reception have since become the stock-in-trade of postcolonial studies in universities worldwide, though theorists have tended to restrict themselves to works originally written in English, among them those by Anglo-Indian novelists such as Salman Rushdie, as well as works written for European audiences, such as those by Frantz Fanon.[24] In addition to questions of representation should be added the study of translation as such; in other words, of the movement of texts across cultural and linguistic boundaries. Postcolonial studies have done this through an emphasis on hybridity, the creative mixing of forms and languages, but there is another academic field devoted to questions of translation alone, and Arabic literature makes an intriguing subject for anyone working in 'translation studies', as it is hoped that this chapter has suggested.[25]

A second approach relevant to reading modern Arabic literature is the study of 'world literature', recently associated with continental European critics such as Franco Moretti and Pascale Casanova. The former's 'Conjectures on World Literature' in particular put the study of literary geography back on the map, as it were, substituting what he called 'units that are much smaller or much larger than the text' such as 'devices, themes, tropes – or genres and systems' for individual novels, plays or poems.

'If the text disappears,' Moretti wrote, 'it is one of those cases when one can justifiably say, less is more. If we want to understand the system in its entirety, we must accept losing something.' The 'system'

Moretti had in mind was the 'literary world system', modelled in terms of centre and peripheries using language taken from economics. The same author's later pieces have sought to show how his proposed 'graphs, maps and trees' can be used to understand the spread of literary forms such as the novel from their origins in Europe to the rest of the world, drawing out lines of extension from a mass of detail.[26]

Casanova has examined similar issues in her book *La République mondiale des lettres*.[27] She again proposed the existence of a 'literary world system', this time modelled in terms of nations competing for dominance within it. Why had Goethe originally shown interest in the notion of 'world literature', for example? Because he lived 'precisely at the moment when Germany was entering international literary space' at the beginning of the nineteenth century and was contesting the 'intellectual and literary hegemony' of France. A country finding itself at the margins of Casanova's system has the option of trying to build up its literary 'capital' and seek out areas of comparative advantage. The system thus has its own form of dynamism, born of competition. Furthermore, writers coming from peripheral areas can draw up strategies for entry and even dominance. According to Casanova, Joyce and Beckett, for example, damned by provinciality, entered the international literary system by adopting the latest aesthetic innovations, thereby gaining recognition. While this came at the price of cutting themselves off from their local Irish roots and audiences, it nevertheless meant that they were able to build up enough prestige to bring about a change of taste among those local audiences.

Casanova's book is marvellously inventive. Some of the 'strategies' used by the Irish, Latin American, Bulgarian, Czech and other writers she considers in their attempts to conquer international literary space can be seen as reminiscent of those used by Arab authors, either in their decisions to become 'international' writers or to remain purely 'local' ones.

The Modern Element

The advent of modernity in the Arab world has traditionally been given a precise date. Although the picture of the historical development of Arab societies of which this date is a part has since been modified, if not rejected, there is still some justice in supposing that the French invasion and occupation of Egypt in 1798, lasting until French forces were driven out by the English three years later, was a crucial event both in the development of Egyptian society and in that of Middle Eastern and Arab societies more generally. This is so because France's brief adventure in the Middle East decisively changed the region's relationship with Europe.

What changed above all in that relationship was the Arab world's insulation from European politics and from the strategic calculations of the European powers. Noting that Egypt was likely to become increasingly important to British interests in India, the French sent their most promising young general, Napoleon Bonaparte, to Egypt at the head of invading forces. While the main aim of this was to 'chase the English from their possessions in the Orient,' as Talleyrand, French foreign minister, put it at the time, the invasion also had other, subsidiary aims. These included liberating the country from 'Mamluk tyranny', re-establishing Ottoman control in the country with the help of France, and taking the ideas of the French Revolution eastwards. As Napoleon put it in a declaration, 'the Genius of Freedom, which has made the French Republic the arbiter of Europe, now desires that it should be so for the most distant seas and countries,' including Egypt and other parts of the Middle East.[1]

Whether the emphasis is put on French revolutionary altruism, or on a desire to frustrate English power, from this date onwards Egypt, the Eastern Mediterranean, and, with it, the Ottoman Empire of which most Arab countries were then a part, were increasingly subject to European intervention. In short, the famous 'Eastern Question' that was to bedevil nineteenth-century diplomacy had begun, and the European powers began to jockey for position amongst themselves, hoping to make gains in the Middle East at each other's expense, as well as at that of the Ottomans and other local rulers. Ideas originating in Europe, notably modern nationalism, began to gain a foothold, and in the wake of European influence came direct colonial control. Algiers was occupied by French forces in 1830, and by 1847 the hinterland had been brought under French rule. Tunisia was declared a French protectorate in 1881. Egypt was occupied by the British in 1882. Morocco became a French protectorate in 1912. Libya was annexed by Italy also in 1912. Following the break-up of the Ottoman Empire after the First World War, Syria, Lebanon, Palestine, Trans-Jordan and Iraq, all of which had been Ottoman provinces until 1918, were 'mandated' to France and Britain, respectively, by the new League of Nations. All this indicates the background of colonialism and dependency against which modern Arabic literature at least at first was written. (Syria and Lebanon went to France, Palestine, trans-Jordan, and Iraq to Britain.)[2]

Yet, while European influence in the Arab world sooner or later led to direct European control, it also led to the modernization of Arab societies along lines suggested by the encounter with Europe. In Egypt, for example, a new, explicitly modernizing regime came to power in 1805 following the French invasion. Led by a former Ottoman soldier of Albanian origin, Mohamed Ali, this regime focused on modernizing state and society in an effort to 'catch up' with the Europeans in ways being tried at the same time by the Ottoman government in Istanbul. The first Egyptian educational missions were sent to Europe in the 1820s in order to learn from European science and technology; the army was reorganized, as were the state institutions; new schools and educational establishments were founded. Modernization also took place elsewhere in the region. In the countries of the Fertile Crescent (roughly speaking the Levant and Iraq), for example, under tighter Ottoman control, it began in earnest with the *tanzimat* (reforms) as the authorities in Istanbul attempted to shake up what was then a notoriously ramshackle way of doing things in the Arab provinces of the empire. In the Maghreb, Algeria was brought under French control, destroying pre-colonial society. Local dynasties in Morocco, and, especially, Tunisia, also set out on the path of modernization and reform.[3]

In short, the nineteenth century was the period of the 'Arab rediscovery of Europe', as a well-known work on the period has it,[4] and while it was a period that revealed Ottoman and Arab inferiority with regard to European economic and military power and technology, it also suggested ways in which this could be made up for through the adoption of European ways. However, this adoption, though laudably meant, was also fraught with dangers. Not only could it lead to the development of an increasingly polarized society, part of which was 'modern' and looked towards Europe, and part of which remained 'traditional' and distrusted the new, foreign ways, but it could also call the foundations of that society as a whole into question. Should Arab societies remain 'traditional', for example, and reject the modern ways in an attempt to safeguard their identity, or should they become 'modern' and transform themselves on a European pattern at the risk of losing some of the things that made them most themselves? Was there perhaps a third possibility: that the 'rebirth' of Arab societies would come about through their modernization along lines suggested by Europe after a long period of Ottoman domination? It was this third possibility that was explored by the pioneering writers of the modern period. While questions of this sort probably confronted all societies at the time that either fell under the influence of Europe or were colonized by one or other of the European states, in the Arab world they gave rise to particularly acute debates.

By the beginning of the twentieth century, questions about tradition and modernization and about what was authentic and what was foreign in national life had become part of the common currency of Arab intellectual debate, with modernizers wanting to bring Arab societies into line with Europe and traditionalists insisting on the primacy of inherited patterns of thought. While the modernists had mostly been educated in the new institutions, either those set up by modernizing regimes such as in Egypt, or in the mission schools and other institutions set up by foreigners, for example in Lebanon, this was by no means always the case. One of the outstanding figures of the age, the Egyptian writer and intellectual Taha Hussein, for example, was educated at al-Azhar in Cairo, according to the traditional religious curriculum. The story of his absorption of that curriculum and subsequent study in France makes one of the most fascinating life-stories in any language. Hussein's accumulation of the 'treasures of popular lore and traditional sciences', his rediscovery of 'a more vital and vigorous past' than that offered at al-Azhar, and his falling 'under the spell of Westernization' are parts of a representative intellectual trajectory from an age that described itself as marking the 'rebirth' (*nahda*), or 'enlightenment' of Arab societies and culture.[5] This rebirth, Hussein and other writers of his generation thought, would come about as a result of a renewed interest and pride in the Arab past and a desire to emulate the modern achievements of the Europeans.

Born in 1889 to a poor rural family, and afflicted by blindness from an early age, Hussein attended village school before registering, in 1902, at al-Azhar in Cairo. This institution, founded a thousand years earlier, was primarily a theology college at the time, training young men in religion. By the time that Hussein attended it, it had fallen into decay, its curriculum

4. The Egyptian writer Taha Hussein, known as the 'Dean of Arabic Literature'

fossilized and it having been outflanked by modern institutions that offered superior career options. Indeed, Hussein says in the first volume of his autobiography, *An Egyptian Childhood*, part of what was to become a three-volume work entitled *The Days*,[6] that his elder brother, who died tragically young of cholera, was destined for medical school, not al-Azhar. While al-Azhar still enjoyed prestige as a centre of traditional and religious culture, though perhaps chiefly in rural areas, its graduates no longer played a major role in the modern economy or in the professions.

Hussein, a 'young sheikh', managed, mostly successfully, to memorize the *Qur'an* by the time he was nine years old, though not without the sometimes comic lapses of memory recorded in his autobiography. He was a sensitive, solitary child, and perhaps it was thought that, being blind, his best chance of a job would be as an assistant in a religious school. However, if this was the case he was to prove such ideas wrong, going on to become Rector of Cairo University, Egyptian Minister of Education and one of the most important representatives of the country's modern intelligentsia that tried to find an accommodation between traditional values and developing modern ways, while at the same time working towards a more sophisticated conception of tradition and the renovation of Arab literary culture.

In *The Stream of Days,* for example, Hussein gives a fascinating account of student life at al-Azhar in the early years of the twentieth century and the hopes he invested in his education. As a result of being separated from his peers by his blindness, the young boy's solitude comes across strongly, as does his poverty, as he lies awake at night listening to various creatures scratching about in the walls of his lodgings. However, Hussein also often refers to Mohamed Abdu, who had been a leading teacher at the institution shortly before and had engaged in a struggle for its modernization and for the renovation of religious culture more generally. Hussein's sympathies clearly lie with 'the Imam', and his memoirs are full of references to the uselessness of many of the al-Azhar teachers at the time, together with his contempt for the atmosphere of 'intrigue, backbiting, [and] imposture' that reigned in the institution.[7]

Rebelling against the 'gross taste and jaded wits of the Azhar', Hussein turned away from the official curriculum and towards the study of classical Arabic literature, falling under the influence of men seeking to renovate and develop the country's intellectual life within the framework of Egyptian and Arab nationalism. He also started to contribute articles to the newspapers of the day. 'I know of nothing in the world which can exert so strong an influence for freedom, especially on the young, as literature,' Hussein writes, remembering his efforts to escape from what seemed to him to be the narrow limits of traditional learning as conceived of at al-Azhar. He had, he says, a 'long-cherished dream of entering the lay world of the *tarboush*' at a time 'when he was sick to death of the turban and all that it implied.' (Hussein writes in the third person throughout his autobiography, though translations do not always preserve this.) While the '*tarboush*', or '*fez*', was part of a modern style of dress, representing the styles of thought then being sought from Europe, the turban represented the traditionalist mentality incarnated by al-Azhar, which, in Hussein's view, was urgently in need of renovation.

If there is a single leading theme in Hussein's autobiography, then it is the broadening of horizons that came about with the widening of his own education, first at al-Azhar, then at the new Egyptian University founded in 1908 along European lines, and then at university in France. By the end of volume two of his memoirs, Hussein has joined the Egyptian University. In the third volume, entitled *A Passage to France* and not published until the year of Hussein's death in 1973, he describes the new forms of teaching and learning that he found there, as well as the developing ambitions these awoke in him. 'I would come to hold the place in Egypt that Voltaire had occupied in France,' he writes, staging himself as, like Voltaire, a 'bringer of enlightenment' – the translation of the Arabic expression – or at least as a kind of critical gadfly to traditionalist mentality. Hussein's determination, as well as what must have been his unusual energy and resourcefulness, then took him to study at the Sorbonne in Paris, submitting a thesis on the medieval Arab historian Ibn Khaldoun that was supervised by Durkheim.

Hussein's experiences are relevant to the creation of modern Arabic literature in the early decades of the twentieth century because they express not only the idea of the 'rebirth' of Arab culture through the renovation of tradition and through contact with European ideas, but also the adoption of European literary forms and of a liberal idea of literature. Hussein is sometimes credited with writing the 'first' modern autobiography in Arabic in *The Days*, for example, and other members of his generation are referred to as 'pioneers', being responsible for the first novel, the first short stories and the first plays written in Arabic. Moreover, these works, heavily influenced by the translation into Arabic of European novels, plays and other materials at the time, held out the possibility of giving new purpose to literature in general. While this was, or could be, a source of entertainment, as perhaps it had traditionally been in Arab societies in which literary writing was admired above all for the writer's skills, it could also serve as a form of veiled instruction and as a vehicle for the articulation of social themes, as had been the case, for example, in the nineteenth-century European novel. There was a marked connection with the development of national consciousness. Conditions for the emergence of the pioneering works written by members of Hussein's generation are picked out below, together with various works and authors.

A first condition for the growth of a modern literature was the existence of a new intellectual class, educated at European-style institutions or in modern ways and desiring to create a literature in Arabic on the European model. These men would wear the *tarboush*, rather than the turban. As has been seen, Hussein identified himself as a member of that class, and his impatience with traditionalist ways is often palpable. In addition, new forms of publication were required, as was the education of a reading public, the latter ideally sharing the high values the new generation of writers projected onto the new literature, even if it was sometimes slow to read it. The first of these two requirements at least was met by the development of Arabic newspapers in the later decades of the nineteenth century, often by Lebanese entrepreneurs, which provided a forum for debate. Hussein, for example, describes his early experiences as a journalist in *The Stream of Days*, writing for the magazine *al-Garida*. Finally, the period also saw the development of a recognizably modern intellectual milieu, which now began to organize itself into groups with common aims and around group publications, in a manner familiar from the development of many intellectual avant-gardes.[8]

However, beyond all these things the period was one of excited political debate, fuelled by the rise of nationalism and the possibility that the Arabs, having detached themselves from Ottoman rule, whether slowly as in Egypt, or as a result of the dismemberment of the Ottoman Empire following the First World War, were now both rediscovering their heritage and building a future of national self-rule for themselves. In Egypt, this debate culminated in the 1919 Revolution against British rule, though this was by no means the end of British colonialism in the country. Elsewhere, things were much less satisfactory, with the former Arab territories of the Ottoman Empire being divided under British and French colonial control under a system of League of Nations 'mandates' and having to wait decades for independence. Nevertheless, various forms of literary and cultural experiment were a part of the nation-building process, and by the 1920s conditions were in place for the growth and flourishing of modern Arabic literature.[9]

One important group of early writers is the so-called 'Modern School' that grew up in Egypt in the 1920s. Members of this group included Mahmoud Taymour, whose short stories, modelled on those of Maupassant, gave Egyptian content to an originally European form that had now begun to flourish in the new newspapers, and, a little later, Yahya Hakki, editor of the group's house journal *al-Fajr* ('The Dawn') which served as a showcase for these writers' work. Hakki in particular played an important role in the development of modern Arabic literature, both at this early stage and much later in the 1950s and 1960s when he had retired from his extra-literary career as a diplomat. He is the author of a novella, *The Lamp of Umm Hashim*,[10] which is often considered a representative text from this early period.

The Lamp of Umm Hashim describes the experiences of a young man,

Ismail, who is impatient with his own society, having been educated as a medical doctor in Europe. Yet, while he at first rejects his own country, describing it on his return from Europe as 'a sprawling piece of mud that has dozed off in the middle of the desert', he later comes to see that the contrast between modern science, rational habits of thought, and economic and political development, all represented in his eyes by Europe, and superstition, backwardness and poverty, all qualities he projects upon his own society, is not as clear cut as he had at first imagined. At the end of the story he is reconciled both with himself and with his society.

The story is thus a kind of moral fable that illustrates possible consequences of the Arab encounter with Europe and with the ideas of scientific and social progress that the latter appeared to represent in Arab eyes. Ismail's foreign education is made possible by the sacrifices of his family, the older generation 'annihilating itself so that a single member of its progeny might come into being', but when he returns from Europe and looks at the Cairo district in which he was born and grew up he sees only chaos and a superstitious population that 'makes[s] pilgrimages to graves and ... seek[s] refuge with the dead.' The district is built around the Mosque of Sayeda Zeinab, and a lamp, the lamp of Umm Hashim (another name for Sayeda Zeinab), hangs above her shrine.[11] The lamp contains oil believed to have healing properties because of its religious associations, and Ismail is appalled to discover that his mother has been using it to treat the eyes of a young woman to whom he had been engaged to be married. 'You should be ashamed of yourself at the harm you're doing,' he shouts. 'How can you accept such superstition and humbug?'

Ismail begins to treat Fatima's condition according to the lights of modern medicine instead. Going to the shrine, he sees the lamp of Umm Hashim, 'its thin ray of light ... a standing advertisement to superstition and ignorance,' the shrine itself surrounded by people 'like wooden props, paralysed, clinging to its railings.' He raises his stick and smashes the lamp, believing that in doing so he is 'delivering a *coup de grâce* to the very heart of ignorance and superstition' and that he is hauling, if necessary by force, his countrymen out of the past and into the modern world. Unsurprisingly, his gesture is misread, and he is set upon by visitors to the shrine. He suffers from a kind of psychological breakdown, made no better by the fact that the treatment he is giving Fatima does not improve her condition. 'Who can deny Europe's civilization and progress, and the ignorance, disease, and poverty of the East,' Ismail asks himself. However, though he has returned from Europe 'with a large quiver stuffed with knowledge', this proves insufficient in Egypt. Slowly he comes to realize that some kind of reconciliation with the past is necessary, the novella indicating that an attitude of respect for the past and for the traditional ways of life and thought that have emerged from it will make Ismail both a better doctor and a better human being. Going back to medicine, he cures Fatima's eye disease and opens a clinic in a poor Cairo district, where he performs operations 'using methods that would have left a European doctor aghast', relying 'first and foremost upon God, [and] then on his knowledge and the skill of his hands.'

Perhaps best read as a lesson in humility rather than as an attack on science, *The Lamp of Umm Hashim* reflects on identity and on the need to act in continuation with the past rather than reject it by imitating Europe. However imperfect the inherited culture may be, the novella seems to be saying, it is a part of Ismail's own past and his own identity. At the end of the novella Ismail seems to have found an accommodation between the 'Egyptian' and the 'European' sides of his personality, the one representing traditional culture and the other new ideas, including scientific ideas, just as the former represents family and community and the latter individual ambition. While dualisms of this kind were already staples of intellectual debate, Hussein's autobiography suggesting a different kind of accommodation, for

5. Egyptian playwright and man of letters Tawfiq al-Hakim, one of the 'pioneers' of modern Arabic literature

example, to substantially the same dilemmas, Hakki's novella is a concise representation of his generation's thinking. This, it might be thought, aimed at the modernization of Arab culture without changing its essential character or severing its roots in tradition.[12]

Other important works by this pioneering generation include those by the Egyptian novelist and playwright Tawfiq al-Hakim, whose prose works make fascinating reading for anyone interested in the development of a modern literary milieu in the Arab world, with all its rivalries, financial worries and promises of fame and fortune.

The son of a prominent lawyer, al-Hakim himself disliked the law and early on began to dream of writing plays for the nascent Egyptian theatre. However, like many playwrights before and since he discovered that 'serious' drama does not pay, particularly in a commercial theatre world where song-and-dance routines seemed to be the norm, and his frustrations are recorded in his many volumes of autobiography, among them *The Prison of Life*.[13] In this volume, published in Arabic in 1964, al-Hakim looks back on a career spent in the theatre. Like Hussein and Hakki, al-Hakim studied in Europe, though probably with less application, and during a period spent in Paris he immersed himself in the literature of the time, starting to write plays in a new style informed by fashionable dramatists like

Pirandello on his return to Egypt. Al-Hakim's theatre work is discussed later. For present purposes, two works from the early 1930s, the novels *Return of the Spirit* and *Diary of a Country Prosecutor*, will be examined.[14] Had al-Hakim not gone on to write anything else apart from these two works, his place in Arabic letters would be secure on the strength of them.

Written while al-Hakim was himself a lawyer in the Egyptian Delta, *Diary of a Country Prosecutor*, like many works both before and since, capitalizes on the comic possibilities offered by the law. Apparently a murder mystery, though one that is never solved, the novel records the frustrations of a minor official sent out from Cairo into the alien world of the Egyptian peasantry, his instructions being to enforce the law. That law, however, is alien to the villagers with whom he deals, and the life of the anonymous public prosecutor in the novel is not made any easier by the habits of his fellow officials. One judge, in the job too long and used to cutting corners, gets through a day's cases in a couple of hours; another, of a more anxious disposition, insists on every document in every case being perfect, stretching hearings long into the evenings at the expense of the prosecutor's much-needed rest. In the face of such abuses, the novel's anonymous narrator reflects on the absurdity of his situation, being condemned to listen to sentences being passed on illiterate villagers much in the manner of the Queen in

Alice in Wonderland. However, he also reflects on his activity as a writer, and what this might entail in a society where the vast majority of the population can neither read nor write. 'By nature I am fitted to be a hidden observer of people strutting across the stage of life,' he writes, but for all that he is an observer who has a responsibility to record, and to protest against, the injustices that he sees around him. Literature, in the hands of Hakki and al-Hakim, thus served both to dramatize the dilemmas of a rapidly modernizing society that seemed in danger of losing its moorings and to expose the social injustices suffered by the population.

Such issues receive more ample treatment in al-Hakim's longer novel *Return of the Spirit.* This work, published in Arabic in 1933, is a less approachable, probably less successful, work in translation than the *Diary*, though it is one that once again draws upon al-Hakim's gift for observation, as well as on his own experiences, this time of his student days in Cairo. It is a humorous, even slapstick, work. However, the novel also broaches explicitly nationalist themes, and it is said to have been favourite reading of Nasser, later president of the republic established in Egypt following that country's 1952 Revolution. In this novel, al-Hakim suggests that the fight against British occupation, which had reached its climax in 1919, should be seen as part of a 'return of the spirit' of the nation, in other words of a kind of general awakening after years of slumber. It was part of the general renovation of Egyptian society after centuries of first Ottoman and then British rule. For these reasons, the novel, much like the works of Hussein or Hakki, is often seen as an important statement of the Arab *nahda*, or renaissance, if in a provincial Egyptian form.

Much of the novel is set in Cairo, where the protagonist, Muhsin, is a student lodging with his extended family in a tiny flat in the crowded district of Sayeda Zeinab. However, the episodes that concern us here take place later in volume two of the novel, when Muhsin travels outside Cairo to the Nile Delta. On the train from Cairo, for example,

Muhsin falls into conversation with the other passengers in his compartment, a veritable cross-section of Egyptian society, and the conversation turns to the differences between Egyptian and European society. In Egypt, the passengers agree, 'kinship and spiritual solidarity' are important values. Europeans, by contrast, have sacrificed these to 'efficiency', competition and dog-eat-dog individualism. Al-Hakim thereby returns to the theme, familiar from works by Hussein and Hakki, of the possible differences between Arab and European societies, pointing to the allegedly soulless materialism of the one and the greater spiritual satisfactions to be had in the other. Yet, even more striking than this assertion of national unity built in opposition to European values is a later discussion between an Egyptian landowner, a British irrigation inspector and a French archaeologist, the latter two imported into the novel for the occasion. The French archaeologist begins a disquisition on the rural labourers he sees around him, contrasting their present poverty to a 'force within them that they are not conscious of'. This 'force', or 'spirit', is the legacy of the ancient Egyptians, he says, and it explains 'those moments of history during which we see Egypt take an astonishing leap in only a short time and work wonders in the wink of an eye.' Don't be surprised, he says, if these people, who stand together as one and who relish sacrifice, bring forth another miracle besides that of the pyramids.

Though rather crudely inserted into the novel, this is a striking statement of national rebirth and of the heights that will be reached once the nation has been rid of ignorance, illiteracy and foreign domination. It represents the hopes of an entire generation.[15]

Works by Hussein, Hakki and al-Hakim are among the 'classics' of modern Arabic literature, these three writers being leading members of the generation that is often seen as having established it. However, these men wrote in prose, and this can obscure the fact that the poetry and drama of the time were also concerned with questions of identity and with the renovation of Arab society and the building of national consciousness. Poetry and drama also had a different status from prose writing, with poetry being perhaps the most prestigious of all Arab literary forms and drama perhaps the least.

Unlike prose fiction, poetry was not a recently developed form or one of foreign origin, and it is still sometimes referred to as the form of writing that best expresses the literary genius of the Arabs. However, poetry too was believed to have fallen into decay during the long centuries of Ottoman rule, and it was therefore also due for renovation. Various solutions to the form that this might take were considered. While 'neo-classical' poets like Ahmed Shawqi and Hafez Ibrahim in Egypt experimented with introducing new subject matter into poetry written in classical language and in traditional forms, the 'Romantic' and *Mahjar* poets used a simpler vocabulary and simpler forms and placed the emphasis more on subjective experience than on virtuoso display. (*Mahjar* means emigrant, these poets having emigrated, usually to the United States, from Syria or Lebanon: Gibran, encountered in Chapter 1, is an example.)

Both Shawqi, the 'prince of poets', and Ibrahim are firmly installed in the canon of modern Arabic poetry, and familiarity with their works is essential for any educated speaker of Arabic. This means that acquaintance with them is often made at school and seldom renewed in later life. For the foreign reader things are made more complicated by the absence of accessible translations of these poets' work, and it is easy to gain an idea of Shawqi or Ibrahim as impressive, if rather dilapidated, poetic monuments, rather like Victorian poets such as Tennyson. In fact, however, both Shawqi and Ibrahim played a significant role in giving new subject matter to Arabic poetry, introducing social and political themes to it together with a marked nationalist component and following in the footsteps of the earlier nationalist poet Mahmoud Sami al-Baroudi (who had also been a prime minister of Egypt). Thus, while in formal and linguistic terms they opted for a 'return to sources', setting out 'to bridge the gap of long centuries of immobility' by a return to medieval models, in the words of one critic,[16] theirs was not entirely a poetry of pastiche. Encased in all the medieval flummery there was a core message of national and cultural origins; the antique style, while implausible in the context of the 1920s, could at least suggest a story of historical continuity. Shawqi wrote a large amount of 'occasional' poetry, for example, befitting his position as court poet to the aristocracy, including a 1904 panegyric to the Khedive, ruler of Egypt at the time, and 'Tutankhamun', which ends on a note of praise for the Egyptian King Fu'ad. The latter is a 'poem about the fate of a nation', in which Shawqi draws connections between past glories, represented by the discovery of the ancient Pharoah's tomb, and present possibilities. Similarly, Ibrahim in poems such as 'Hailing the Muslim Year' writes public poetry commenting on current events. In Ottoman Turkey, for example, 'the constitutionalists [have] made a breakthrough', while in Iran 'the wicked Shah is still at the helm'. In Egypt, by contrast, 'the days of slumber are gone and a new spirit has animated the Egyptian nation.'

The 'Romantic' and '*Mahjar*' poets, emerging on the poetic scene a little later, took a different view of modern Arabic poetry, and they jettisoned both the public themes and classical language adopted by Shawqi and Ibrahim in favour of a simpler, lyric style designed to convey the poet's emotions. Romantic poets such as the members of the 'Diwan School' in Egypt, among whom are Ibrahim Abdel-Qader al-Mazini and Abbas Mahmoud al-Aqqad, together with Ilya Abu Madi, a *Mahjar* poet, and Abu al-Qasim al-Shabbi in Tunisia, and the slightly later Egyptian 'Apollo School', 'achieved nothing less than a revolution in the language of poetry and in general poetic sensibility.'[17] As a result, they 'introduced a vital phase of flexibility and experimentation into both form and metre which prepared the way for the prosodic transformations of the late 1940s and early 1950s', creating 'nothing less than a new language of poetry in Arabic'.These later transformations are discussed in Chapter 3.

Finally, a major source for the drama of this early period is al-Hakim's memoirs, notably *The Prison of Life*. In this book al-Hakim gives a picture both of the pioneers discussed in this chapter and of his own early thinking, for example that behind the writing of *Return of the Spirit* ('an effort it was my duty to exert, to the development of the genre' of the novel in Arabic). He describes the condition of Arab theatre as he found it in Cairo in the 1910s and 1920s, with originally Lebanese impresarios, such as Georges Abyad, 'Egyptianizing' or 'Arabizing', in other words loosely 'translating', European plays for Arab audiences. This was a process that could lead to some fascinating conundrums: 'when adapting a foreign play in which a man and a woman met, we were getting into a can of worms. How could we put on an Egyptian stage a man and a woman face to face if they were not related?' (The wearing of the full, 'Turkish' face veil was *de rigeur* for women of the middle and upper classes in Egypt at the time and would remain so until well into the 1920s.)

Wanting to write plays in the manner of 'Ibsen, Pirandello, Bernard Shaw, [and] Maeterlinck', al-Hakim found himself without an audience and in need of a 'serious theatrical environment'. 'The fact is,' he writes, that 'literature and a career solely in it were not taken seriously in a society that gave respect, prestige, and wealth only to Pashas [aristocrats] or to men of authority and position in government.' This complaint is echoed by Naguib Mahfouz in his portrait of Kamal, a struggling journalist and writer to whom he bears more than a passing resemblance, in the second and third volumes of his *Cairo Trilogy*. Many things would change when states across the Arab world began seriously to support the arts following the end of colonial rule after the Second World War, though with sometimes mixed results, as we shall see.

The Novel and the New Poetry

Political circumstances in the Arab world in the decades following the end of the Second World War were in some ways propitious and in some ways unpropitious for literature. The end of European colonial control in the 1950s meant that greater stress than ever before was laid on the development of education and culture. This could not help but be positive for literature, and many Arab writers welcomed the removal of regimes linked to the colonial order, for example in Egypt in 1952 or Iraq in 1958. However, with the new regimes came new pressures on Arab writers. Not only did the revolutionary regimes insist upon the support of writers and intellectuals, but those who did not support the new regimes could expect censorship or worse. As the decades wore on, and the hopes that the new regimes had given rise to were either disappointed or defeated, it became clear that though there were now more professional writers than ever, together with a great deal more money to support them, their lives were in many respects scarcely easier than they had been before.

Some of these pressures can be seen in the career of the giant of the writing of the post-war period and of modern Arabic literature more

7. Naguib Mahfouz, the greatest of all Arab novelists

generally, the late Egyptian novelist Naguib Mahfouz. No introduction to the subject would be complete without extended consideration of his work, and non-Arabic-speaking readers are fortunate in that almost all of Mahfouz's work in book form has been translated into European languages, including much of his juvenilia, journalism and other writings. Mahfouz, unlike almost any other modern Arab writer, and unlike even figures of the stature of those discussed in the previous chapter, can thus be seen in the round by non-Arabic-speaking readers and his career appreciated as a whole.

Born in 1911 to a middle-class family in Cairo, Mahfouz graduated from Cairo University, then called Fu'ad 1 University, in 1934 with a degree in Philosophy, and he seems at first to have intended to follow an academic career. However, instead he joined the Egyptian civil service, eventually retiring nearly four decades later. Following a period in which he experimented with historical novels, he found his true subject in the lives of the Cairo lower and lower-middle-classes. Early novels such as *Midaq Alley* and *The Beginning and the End* demonstrated a commitment to realism,[1] dwelling in particular on the explosive social inequalities of the post-war years. A decade later, in 1956, Mahfouz published his greatest work, the *Cairo Trilogy* of *Palace Walk, Palace of Desire* and *Sugar Street,* novels that trace the life of a Cairo family across successive generations from the early decades of the twentieth century to the late 1940s against a background of social change.² This work, almost unparalleled in its scope and richness in modern Arabic literature, established Mahfouz as the major novelist of his generation.

While Mahfouz was to live for a further five decades, later establishing himself as a leading experimentalist, the *Cairo Trilogy* is perhaps his single most important achievement. One reason for this is its ambition and scope: running to over 1,200 pages in the omnibus edition, the work allows the novelist to record historical events from the nationalist agitation against the British in the early decades of the century in volume one, to the politics and pre-revolutionary disturbances following the Second World War in volume three, making the work a primary source for Egyptian history and the development of Arab society. However, beyond this perhaps Mahfouz's achievement in the *Trilogy* lies in his having produced an Arabic novel that unites the European form of the realist novel with local Egyptian content, exploring the public, and perhaps even more importantly, the private, lives of his characters in unprecedented detail. Rather like the characters created by the great nineteenth-century European novelists, such as Dickens or Flaubert, these characters have since detached themselves from their author's control and entered the culture in their own right.³

Few readers are likely to forget the character of Ahmad Abd al-Jawad, 'so wealthy, strong, and handsome, who stayed out night after night' on various jaunts, or that of his wife, Amina, waiting patiently for him at home, in volume one of the *Trilogy*. Nor are they likely to be blind to the careful way in which the characters of the couple's children, Fahmy, Yasin (Amina's stepson), Kamal, Khadija and Aisha are drawn. Episodes from this novel, such as Amina's visit to the Mosque of al-Husayn accompanied by her youngest son Kamal, causing her to be temporarily expelled from the family home, have something of the same standing in Arab culture as, say, Pip's visits to the aged Miss Havisham in Dickens's *Great Expectations* have in

English. Mahfouz has Amina explain ironically to her son, a portrait of the author, that there is nothing wrong in his not being as good-looking as his brothers, or in his having a head that is out of all proportion to his body. Had not the martyred head of al-Husayn, the young boy asks himself before his trip to the mosque with his mother, 'after being severed from his immaculate body, chose[n] Egypt from all the world for its resting place? Immaculate, it came to Cairo, glorifying God, and settled to the ground where al-Husayn's shrine now stands.'[4]

Few readers, either, are likely to forget the elegant way in which characters and relationships established in volume one are developed in the two following volumes, or the way in which Mahfouz skilfully mixes personal tragedy with large, public themes, such as occurs with the death of Fahmy during anti-British demonstrations at the end of volume one. 'Who could have imagined this,' Fahmy asks himself before his death at the hands of British soldiers. 'There's never been a demonstration like this before. A hundred thousand people, wearing modern fezzes and traditional turbans – students, workers, civil servants, Muslim and Christian religious leaders, the judges ... This is Egypt.' This Egypt, complicated enough in 1919, though temporarily united against the British, has become a good deal more so by the end of volume three of the *Trilogy*, in which the children of volume one now have children of their own. Kamal's own nephews, Ahmad and Abd al-Muni'm Shawkat, for example, are now on opposite sides of the political divide, the former a journalist and member of an illegal leftist party, in which he meets women of the type that his grandmother, illiterate throughout her life, could scarcely have imagined, the latter a member of the Muslim Brotherhood and someone who has directly opposing views of Egyptian identity and society. Both men find themselves in prison at the end of the *Trilogy*.

Following the publication of the *Trilogy*, Mahfouz was silent for several years, only beginning to publish a new novel, *Children of the*

8. For most of his career Nobel laureate Naguib Mahfouz published with the Cairo publisher Maktabat Misr, which gave his books a perhaps misleading visual identity. The cover of Mahfouz's novel *Sugar Street* is pictured

Alley, in the Egyptian newspaper *al-Ahram* in 1959.[5] This, however, marked a new departure, and it began a long period of experiment. For while the *Trilogy* represented one answer to the question of the form the Arabic novel could take, *Children of the Alley* looked for inspiration to religious narrative and to allegory rather than to realism. A kind of history of the world in five chapters, the novel recounts the stories of five main characters, Adham, Gabal, Rifaa, Qassem and Arafa, the first loosely modelled on the story of Adam, expelled by God from Paradise, the four that follow based on the lives of key figures in the Judaeo-Christian and Muslim religious traditions. Gabal, for example, recapitulates the story of Moses, while Rifaa and Qassem draw upon the lives of Jesus and the Prophet Mohamed, respectively. Arafa, for his part, represents modern man whose attitudes are more scientific than religious. Owing in part to its religious content, the novel is, among other things, a fascinating case study of the limits of literary expression in Egyptian and Arab society and how these have changed over time.[6]

Mahfouz's interests shifted again in the 1960s, with the publication of *The Thief and the Dogs* in 1961, the first of what was to become a series of short novels that are very different in form and tone from what had gone before. This novel, like those that followed it, shows the influence of European existentialism, then at its height in the Arab world thanks to the reception given to the work of Sartre. The story of a thief, Said Mahran, who has been released from prison and is now determined to avenge himself on the false friends who helped to send him there, the novel is typical of this phase in Mahfouz's career in its focus on sometimes extreme states of mind, often through the use of internal monologue, and on the predicament of a single character. It was followed by works such as *Autumn Quail*, *The Search*, *The Beggar*, *Adrift on the Nile* and *Miramar*, all short novels, often experimental in form and typically told from the perspective of a first-person narrator, or narrators, whose various predicaments form their subject matter.[7]

In *Autumn Quail*, Mahfouz focuses on Isa ad-Dabbagh, a promising civil servant whose career has been cut short by the purges that followed the 1952 Revolution. Finding himself without a role in life, ad-Dabbagh slowly loses himself in dissipation even as his friends are able to adjust themselves to the new circumstances. There is a similar pattern in *The Search* and *The Beggar*. In the former novel, crime seems to offer a way out of crisis; in the latter, life seems to offer little purpose aside from private gain, particularly when public affairs are firmly under one-party rule. While this is not enough for the novel's main character, Omar al-Hamzawi, a successful lawyer afflicted with a kind of existential malaise, it seems to suit his friends and colleagues well enough. One of these, a successful writer and journalist, advises him to abandon his search for any other purpose in life. 'Be content with popular acclaim and the material rewards,' he tells him. After all, 'the art of our age is simply diversion,' like 'selling popcorn and watermelon seeds.'

The idea that political circumstances, because deeply undemocratic, have removed a sense of purpose from literature is repeated in *Adrift on the Nile*, this novel also suggesting that artists and writers can nevertheless now expect to be rewarded as they never have been before as the ornaments of the regime. A group of professionals – 'the director of an accounts department, an art critic, an actor, an author, a lawyer, a civil servant'– meet regularly on a houseboat on the Nile. 'For the first half of the day we earn our living, and then afterwards we all get into a little boat and float off into the blue'. The novel consists of fragments plucked from this drug-induced haze, these also being recycled as the subject matter for a literary work by one of the characters. Great play is made of the forms that creative work can now take, it having broken with traditional realism, among them the type of experiment associated with 'the Absurd'. The problem is that none of these new options seems to fill the void, either because, the real decisions being made elsewhere, a writer's choices are trivial ones, or because no choice a writer makes will bring him an audience outside the circle of his peers. All of these are, like him, 'adrift on the Nile'. As one of the characters puts it in the earlier novel *The Search*, from 'anti-novel ... to the Theatre of the Absurd ... If you can't attract the public's attention by your profound thoughts, try running naked through [Cairo's] Opera Square'.

Perhaps the best novel Mahfouz wrote during this stage of his career is *Miramar*.[8] Set in a small guesthouse or pension (the 'Miramar') in Alexandria in the 1960s, the novel is divided into five parts, each of which relates the same material from a different character's point of view. While the novel suggests considerable scepticism about the achievements of the 1952 Revolution and the role of the writer under the revolutionary regime, this scepticism is voiced by characters who are themselves in various ways compromised, the author himself disappearing into the background.

For Hosni Allam, a 'gentleman of property' ruined by the Revolution, things are quite clear-cut: '... you don't believe any of this rubbish about socialism and equality. It's simply power ... Have you actually seen any of that gang walking around in poverty lately?' But his views are contextualized both by those of Sarhan el-Beheiry, a member of the Socialist Union, the single party of the time, and by those of Amer Wagdi, a retired liberal journalist. El-Beheiry has done well out of the new order, and he asks his fellow guests to be reasonable: 'look at it this way: what other system could we have in its place? If you think clearly, you'll realize that it has to be either the Communists or the Muslim Brotherhood. Which of those would you prefer ...?' Wagdi, though nostalgic for the pre-revolutionary liberal order and 'living proof that the past was no illusion', reflects that whatever the excesses of the regime's nationalism, one day the city 'had to be claimed by its people,' as a once cosmopolitan Egypt has now been claimed by an aggressively nationalistic regime.

Miramar's display of pluralism might be Mahfouz's way of hedging his bets: a quintessentially liberal writer, his natural bent in this novel is to give a voice to every side without appearing to endorse any. Nevertheless, he tips the scales a little in his treatment of the servant girl, Zohra, a newcomer from the countryside. It was for her, or for people like her, that the Revolution at least in part was made, yet now she appears like 'a faithful dog astray, looking for its master'. She is indifferent to politics, and she is rejected by el-Beheiry following his clumsy attempts to seduce her: what's the good of marrying a girl like Zohra, el-Beheiry asks himself, 'if it doesn't give me a push up the social ladder?' The only character who comes close to Zohra, this lost representative of 'the people', is Amer Wagdi, himself a survival from the pre-revolutionary regime, though Mahfouz does not suggest that nostalgia represents any kind of solution. There is no such easy exit from the Pension Miramar. This novel, hinting at the corruption and murky compromises that characterized life in Egypt in the 1960s, might be compared to *The Man Who Lost His Shadow*, written at the same time by the prolific Cairo journalist and writer Fathy Ghanem. In Desmond Stewart's gripping translation, the latter novel conveys what success under the new regime could involve, and it is told in a similar experimental style.[9]

Among Mahfouz's later novels, *Respected Sir*, *Karnak Café* and *Wedding Song* might be picked out.[10] Each continues the preoccupations of the 1960s, with *Karnak Café* being a *tour de force* of protest against the excesses of the Nasser regime. *Mirrors* is a rewarding work, both in formal terms (it is written in short, named sections, sometimes almost entirely in dialogue), and in terms of its content (a series of sketches of the unnamed narrator's friends and acquaintances, building up into a kind of portrait gallery of the Egyptian middle class). It contains some of the most telling, though typically veiled, indications of Mahfouz's own political and social attitudes.[11] However, in the 1970s Mahfouz's writing also entered a new phase, as he began to experiment with new forms, bringing him close to the experiments carried out at the same date by the younger writers of the 'generation of the 1960s' in Egypt and elsewhere in the Arab world. These are discussed in Chapter 5. While Mahfouz's writings from this time onwards will not strike every reader as being among his best, their consistent search for new forms and subject matter bears witness to a continually exploratory mind. They include works such as *The Harafish*, *Arabian Nights and Days* and *The Journey of Ibn Fattouma*.[12] The first of these, written in the shadow of the riots that broke out in Cairo in January 1977, is often considered Mahfouz's last great work, the disturbances of the time causing him to revisit the theme of the formation of modern Egypt and the connections between the old, pre-modern system and the increasingly troubled modern state. With regard to what might be seen as consistently his best work, on the other hand, published between the 1940s and the 1960s, the foreign reader might well agree with the Iraqi critic who writes that Mahfouz was not only the writer who, more than any other, did the most to develop the Arabic novel, 'rooting' the form in Arab culture, but that he was also in his own way 'the most critical, the most radical and the most subversive of all Arab writers'.[13]

Among Egyptian writers, Mahfouz's greatest rival in the 1950s and 1960s was Yusuf Idris, a short-story writer, dramatist and journalist, whose work compares interestingly with his. Whereas Mahfouz always tended to disappear behind his books, fashioning a self-deprecating public personality, Idris had an arguably closer relationship with the regime and a rather different conception of literature.

Born in 1927 in the Egyptian Delta to a relatively prosperous family, and a medical student in Cairo during the last years of the pre-revolutionary regime, in his work Idris, like Mahfouz, attempted to forge a national literature, though for him this meant a greater focus on the lives of the poor and a more direct approach to the exposure of injustice and hypocrisy. Whereas Mahfouz cultivated an unruffled public image, Idris typically presented himself as a passionate, even angry, man.[14] From his student days onwards, when he was arrested for left-wing political activities, Idris was a more obviously 'committed' writer than Mahfouz, arguing that literature should assist in the process of social change and in the struggle to bring in a more just social order. Like many writers at the time, he welcomed the 1952 Revolution and the collapse of the hated monarchical regime, identifying the agent of social change in the Nasser regime that replaced it. Perhaps inevitably he was disappointed in that regime's actual record, becoming more and more disillusioned in later life and less and less productive in literary terms.

Idris's first collection of short stories, *The Cheapest Nights*, appeared in 1954, and, together with the volumes that swiftly followed it, contains some magnificent stories, some of the best written in Arabic, including 'All on a Summer's Night', 'The Dregs of the City' and 'The Shame', filmed as *The Sin* in 1965 with Egyptian actress Faten Hamama in the lead role. Later pieces that have been widely noticed include the longer stories 'The Stranger' and 'The Black Policeman'.[15] The former story is a study of the psychology of killing, the latter of the effects of torture, not on the tortured but on those doing the torturing.

'All on a Summer's Night' is set in the Egyptian countryside and is the story of a group of boys, farm labourers, who meet by the irrigation canals on summer nights to dream of a better life, or at least of a life not so dominated by toil and sexual and other forms of frustration. 'A handful of boys ... their muddy faces full of cracks, their clothes in rags, their faces an indefinite blur of tanned hide', they dream of going to the nearby town of Mansoura. This dream,

9. Still from the film of *The Sin* by Yusif Idris, made in 1965 with Egyptian actress Faten Hamama in the lead role

however, is no sooner realized than it ends in an outbreak of violence and in the frustrated realization that 'we were wretchedly poor, and that there was nothing in our homes but barking dogs and roaring fathers and screeching mothers and the suffocating smoke of the stove.' 'The Shame' also ends in frustration and defeat. The story of Fatma, a young girl wrongly suspected of breaking the strict honour code that governs sexual behaviour in her village, it shows Fatma being eventually vindicated, though not before horrific violence is done to her.

Idris's description of such modest lives is repeated in 'The Dregs of the City', in which a prim young judge, carried away by the obsequiousness he thinks of as his due, seduces a female servant from a poor area of the city. This he does mainly out of idleness, but also out of a desire to assert his power over her, the story pointing to connections between class difference and sexual exploitation. At the end of the story, the judge seeks out his servant among the 'dregs of the city', suspecting her of having stolen his watch. For a moment he feels ashamed at the performance he is putting on before this miserable woman: standing in the squalor of her home, demanding the return of a cheap watch, he catches a glimpse of the ridiculous figure he cuts. He feels much better when driving back into the better parts of the city, once the 'orderly streets come into view', where the 'people are clean-shaven and well dressed and their features are fine.'

Idris saw his writing as a mode of intervention in contemporary life, which is why, later in his career, he insisted that he could not engage in literary writing with the streets of Cairo flooded with sewage water, public services having broken down as a result of years of mismanagement, and with 'economic anarchy ... rampant'. Instead, he stepped up his activities as a journalist, contributing a regular column to the newspaper *al-Gumhuriyya* throughout the 1960s and to *al-Ahram* from the 1970s onwards. Moreover, Idris wanted to produce a 'truly Egyptian' national literature that should serve as a series of 'revolutionary blasts' against present conditions. He disliked both the 'pale imitation of European literature fashionable in the late forties', consisting of what he saw as the 'aestheticism and the elitist conception of literature still fostered by "grand old men" like Taha Hussein' and the result of the earlier generation's desire to construct modern Arabic literature on the European model. He commented bitterly on what he saw as the 'drudgery' of Mahfouz's *Cairo Trilogy*, for him a sort of vast pastiche of European realism.

However, Idris also disliked the experiments with the Arab 'heritage', in other words with pre-modern literary materials, that other writers were turning to in a desire to produce a literature less contaminated by foreign influences. 'Our cultural heritage is crammed with nonsense,' he wrote, 'so much so that when contemplating those hundreds of thousands of books in the

National Library I curse the day we learnt to write Arabic.' Perhaps Lytton Strachey felt something similar when contemplating what he felt were the cartloads of stuff produced by the British nineteenth-century writers he satirized in *Eminent Victorians*. Perhaps one can see in Idris a figure like Ismail in Hakki's fable *The Lamp of Umm Hashim*, desiring to liberate himself from the past, even at the risk of smashing it entirely, yet at the same time seeing in that past reflections of the deepest parts of his personality.

Idris wrote of the 'huge, strange gulf that separates our written language from the simple and fluent idiom in which we speak', meaning that 'literature', elevated conceptions of which Idris disliked, almost inevitably sounded artificial for reasons explored earlier in this book. This gulf was social as much as intellectual, separating the educated classes from the masses, and Idris dramatizes such issues in his stories, not only in pieces like 'The Dregs of the City', where the realities of the class structure are exposed, but also in those stories where 'preachers, authorities and reform-minded intellectuals ... deliver *ex cathedra* speeches to admiring or stunned peasants ... their grandiloquence [being] only partly understood, if at all.' He had a 'deep-seated dislike of the established literary and linguistic authorities', notably the 'bunch of eccentrics' making up bodies like the Arabic Language Academy, who sometimes spoke in literature's name.[16]

Idris's writings, in their frustrations as well as in their impatience for change, are typical of a strand of Arabic literature in the 1950s and 1960s that insisted on literature having a clear social message and its authors a clear 'commitment' to change. In this respect, Arabic literature was within the international mainstream (this was the decade of the 'Angry Young Men' in Britain), and 'committed' writers like Idris had little time for their elder peers, for whom 'literature is an end in itself'.[17] A typical novel of the period is Abdel Rahman al-Sharqawi's *Egyptian Earth*, well translated by Desmond

Stewart, which focuses on the lives of Egypt's peasant farmers, the *fellaheen*, and protests against their ill-treatment.[18] The poetry of the period displays similar qualities, as explained below.

Outside Egypt, prose writers such as the Sudanese Tayib Salih and the Saudi national Abdelrahman Munif are among the most important writers of the post-war period. Salih came to prominence in the 1960s, and Munif's writing career began in the 1970s, only ending with his death in 2004. Salih's best-known novel, at the time of writing the only work by a modern Arab author to appear in the 'Penguin Classics' series of world literary works, is *Season of Migration to the North*, already referred to above. Other works include a collection of short stories set in Wad Hamid, the same village in the Sudan that features in *Season of Migration*, brought together in English in a volume entitled *The Wedding of Zein*. There is also *Bandarshah*, a later, longer work that represents a development from the world presented in *Season of Migration* and that is Salih's most recent published work.[19]

Born in 1929 in northern Sudan, Salih's professional career led him to posts in various international organizations in Europe and elsewhere, as well as to a great deal of journalism. In his literary writing, he has focused on the relationship between a poor and swiftly developing post-colonial society, in this case the Sudan, and the European society that contains both the former colonial power and represents the promise, or threat, of change. This theme of the meeting of cultures, dramatized through the experiences of either an Egyptian man travelling to Europe, or of Europeans coming to the Arab world, had been mined by others long before Salih turned his attention to it, notably by al-Hakim in *Return of the Spirit*, in which Egypt is compared positively with Europe, and Hakki in *The Lamp of Umm Hashim*.[20] However, Salih's novel, published in Arabic in 1966 ten years after Sudanese independence, gives a new, harder edge to this relationship in its examination of two characters, the anonymous narrator of the novel whose journey to Europe takes place at the beginning of the post-colonial period, and the older figure of Mustafa Sa'eed, who made a similar journey in the 1920s during the period of Anglo-Egyptian colonial rule. Whereas the works of both al-Hakim and Hakki suggest that anxieties raised by the encounter of Europe and the Arab world can be laid to rest in a kind of 'higher synthesis', there being no necessary conflict between traditional ways of thinking and new and foreign ideas, Salih's work is altogether less sanguine. Though written at a time of optimism at the possibilities held out by development in the immediate post-colonial period, *Season of Migration* might nevertheless be understood as a rather bleak, pessimistic work.

One recent critic has suggested that Salih's novels may be seen as 'episodes in a continuous narrative ... that gives full expression to the state of dissolution experienced throughout Arab societies' as a result of European influence, something in the manner of what the Nigerian novelist Chinua Achebe achieved in his *Things Fall Apart*, which describes the decay of traditional society in West Africa following British incursion. All Salih's works show a 'progression from an initial state of peace and being at home in the world to one of profound estrangement or crisis,' often coming about as a result of the impact of foreign rule or ideas. This estrangement has to do with a wider crisis of 'Arab ideology', polarized between a 'vain attempt to mimic the West', broadly speaking the aim of the writers and thinkers associated with the *nahda*, and more recent 'nostalgic call[s] for a "return" to tradition', associated with various 'fundamentalist' thinkers arguably concerned to re-establish what they see as certain basic values after a period of foreign domination.[21]

Thus, in *Season of Migration* Salih's characters, the one the 'prize pupil of the English', the other a specialist in English literature marooned in his own society, are confronted by problems of identity and belonging. Mustafa Sa'eed, a 'westernized' intellectual, is 'a lie', neither truly western, nor, as a result of his 'migration to the north', truly Sudanese. He bricks up his English books and English past in a room of his house, forbidden to visitors in a twist of plot reminiscent of 'Bluebeard's Castle', and attempts to live the life of a simple farmer, apparently eventually committing suicide. The narrator, for his part, is at first convinced that he, at least, is not 'a lie' and that there need be no conflict either between the two sides of his personality, or between traditional society and the new ideas coming from outside. Slowly, however, he identifies himself more and more with Sa'eed, eventually entering the latter's forbidden room. In a striking illustration of the 'crisis' afflicting this society as it attempts to hold together western and traditional ideas, a young woman, Hosna Bint Mahmoud, kills the elderly husband forced on her by her family, leading to a general sense of catastrophe. 'It's the first time anything like this has happened in the village since God created it. What a time of affliction we live in,' comments the narrator's grandfather.

While Salih introduced a new tone to Arabic writing hailing from the rural areas of the Sudan, Munif, too, has focused almost exclusively on the history and society of his own native country, in this case Saudi Arabia. In his best-known work, the multi-volume work published in Arabic in the 1980s as *Cities of Salt*, three volumes of which have been translated into English (*Cities of Salt*, *The Trench* and *Variations on Night and Day*[22]), Munif describes the history of an unnamed society bearing a family resemblance to those in the Gulf or to Saudi Arabia, which in the space of just a few decades has gone from being a partially nomadic society based around desert oases to something like what can be seen today, all thanks to oil. The novels paint a thinly veiled portrait of the history of Arab Gulf society from the 1920s to the present. Before his recent death, Munif was considered to be one of the most controversial

Arab novelists, not only because of the importance of his subject matter, but also because Munif himself was not afraid to offend powerful interests in his presentation of it. He was stripped of his Saudi citizenship and lived most of his later life in Syria, Lebanon or Iraq.

Born in 1933 in Amman of mixed Saudi and Iraqi parentage, Munif worked for much of his life in the oil industry, first in Syria and then in Iraq, experience that stood him in good stead in writing his novels. He was also involved in politics. The first of his literary works, the strangely named *Trees and the Assassination of Marzuq*, appeared in 1973, and in it Munif announced the twin themes that dominate the rest of his fiction: the 'destruction of a rural community and its way of life that had become the experience of so many ordinary Arabs', notably as a result of the coming of the oil industry, and the 'exposure of the rampant corruption and lies that dominate public life in the Arab world'. Trees and villages are destroyed, together with the ways of life that they have sheltered, with corruption and lies emerging to take their place. A second novel, *East of the Mediterranean*, followed in 1976, and in it Munif exposed the use made of torture in some Arab countries at the time, particularly against political prisoners. According to the Egyptian critic Sabry Hafez, from whose essay on Munif the above quotations are taken, *East of the Mediterranean* should be compared to a whole body of work in modern Arabic literature that takes imprisonment and torture as its theme.[23]

However, it is the first of Munif's major themes, the destruction of a rural or nomadic community and its way of life, that marks out *Cities of Salt*, at least its first volume. A short novel, *Endings*,[24] had already moved onto this terrain, focusing in its reconstruction of traditional life in the village of al-Tiba on what its translator describes as the 'values which have survived the passage of time and the events of history, at least up till now'. These traditional values include both a keen sense of the village's ecology and a sense of its communal history, orally transmitted from generation to generation in traditional narrative forms. However, it is precisely these aspects of village life – communal storytelling, remembering, the close relationship with nature – that are most at threat from modern developments. The villagers 'hear the sound of axes smashing into the trunks of dessicated trees, and the whole thing makes them feel as though they are the ones being throttled.' Younger people, returning to the village from the expanding cities nearby, give the villagers 'the impression that they are listening to someone else', not a member of the community, 'or that the city has managed to corrupt them completely and made them talk that way'. One might say that in *Endings* Munif the novelist writes al-Tiba's epitaph, doing much the same thing at greater length for the community of Wadi al-Uyoun in *Cities of Salt*.

An 'outpouring of green amid the harsh, obdurate desert', life in Wadi al-Uyoun is disrupted too, this time by the arrival of foreigners, Americans, who 'certainly didn't come for water'. At first, these newcomers pose no obvious threat: 'the *wadi* has seen and heard more people come through than there are grains of sand' comments Mitel al-Hathal, a leading member of the community, 'and none of them ever left a trace.' However, this time they return, bringing machines, 'huge yellow hulks [that] move along and roar,' with them; watching from the *wadi*'s edge, 'deep inside him[self]' al-Hathal 'knew, when the thunder stopped, that the world had ended.' The villagers are expelled and the village obliterated. Anyone 'who remembers those long-ago days,' the narrator comments, 'when a place called Wadi al-Uyoun used to exist, and a man named Miteb al-Hathal, and a brook, and trees, and a community of people used to exist,' will remember 'the tractors which attacked the orchards like ravenous wolves.' 'How is it possible,' he asks himself, 'for people and places to change so entirely that they lose any connection with what they used to be?'

Later novels in the series leave the rural environment and focus instead on politics. The part played by foreign interests in the transformation of traditional society has been noticed in *Cities of Salt*, and in his following novels, *The Trench* and *Variations on Night and Day*, Munif turns his attention to the ways in which these interests operated. In the latter novel, for example, he begins by remembering the 'dawn of the [twentieth] century – the opening decades,' when 'the great powers,' specifically Britain, 'did not ... have the time to deal with the huge number of small emirs and sheikhs' then ruling the region and therefore put one of them, Khureybit, in charge of the others. In due course the latter becomes a British client, charged with 'protecting the caravan roads, and ... keep[ing] a watchful eye on the neighbours, the Turks and the eastern coast.' Used by the British to further their interests, he prospers and takes over neighbouring territories in a series of wars. In all of this he is tutored by the sinister Hamilton, a British agent, who talks of 'how Britain thought and how people of the desert thought. What Britain wanted ... and what the Sultan wanted. The rest of the time they talked about horses, history, tribal genealogy and the battles of yesteryear,' obscuring political interests behind reassuring clouds of orientalism.

The parallels between the fictional history presented in Munif's novels and the real history of Arabia and the Gulf are explored in detail by Hafez in the essay quoted from above, together with the part Britain, and then the United States, played in it. Both Khureybit and Hamilton have historical parallels. In his final works, Munif turned his attention to Iraq, examining the country's nineteenth-century history when it was a province of the Ottoman Empire in the novel *Land of Darkness* and focusing on what for him was the nefarious role played in it by the British. In *Notes on History and Resistance*, a non-fiction work, he explored twentieth-century Iraqi history from the 1917 British occupation to the present day. In this book he also criticizes the actions of the United States in the country and those of the post-2003 Iraqi governments, in his view 'a collection of stalls selling lies and illusions.'[25] Munif is also the author of a memoir of a childhood spent in the Jordanian capital Amman.[26]

As well as seeing major achievements in the novel and short story, post-war decades also saw a revival and transformation in the fortunes of Arabic poetry. However, while prose writing was dominated by Egyptian writers, developments in poetry tended to take place elsewhere, especially in Iraq and Lebanon.

Poetry, as suggested in Chapter 2 above, has long been considered the *diwan al-'arab*, the 'record of the Arabs', and it did not remain aloof from the changes sweeping the Arab world at the time of the Arab renaissance, or *nahda*. Yet, if the post-war period saw widespread demands for the root-and-branch renovation of Arab societies, leading to political change in many of them and a new conception of prose literature in the vanguard of that change, such demands were perhaps all the more keenly felt in poetry. Whereas prose literature had at best a limited rhetorical role, poetry could be used to address mass audiences directly (though novels, suitably adapted, could still reach large audiences when adapted for films). Partly as a result of this, post-war Arabic poetry saw innovation both in formal terms, leading to the eclipse of traditional metres and verse forms, and in terms of diction, which now became less elaborate and closer to the language that people actually spoke, if still not identical with it. Both these changes reflected changing conceptions of the role of the poet in society and the nature of the poet's audience. Moreover, they reflected, too, a greater openness to European poetry and particularly to the kind of innovations that had earlier been made in it, some Arabic poetry from the 1950s onwards being influenced either by the fragmentation and wide-ranging cultural reference to be found in the works of T. S. Eliot, or by the dislocations of language – Rimbaud's *dérèglement de tous les sens* – familiar from modern French poetry.

These themes can be seen in the 'free verse' movement that dominated post-war Arabic poetry, first in Iraq and then in Lebanon. There was, first of all, the rejection of past poetic practice, with poets such as Nazik al-Mala'ika and Badr Shakir al-Sayyab in Iraq, and the poets associated with the reviews *Shi'r* ('Poetry') and *al-ʿAdab* ('Literatures') in Lebanon, casting off inherited forms and diction in favour of poetry that was more direct and could speak to large audiences and not just to the elites that might traditionally have interested themselves in literature. Together with this emphasis on a new language and forms for poetry, 'freeing' it from the traditional constraints of Arabic verse, there was a call for subject matter that was more engaged with social themes, even if the poet's individual voice was often as much in evidence as ever, some post-war poets continuing to achieve 'celebrity' status across the Arab world. Poetry was now often seen as a natural part of a 'committed' literature calling for social change. Finally, there were calls for the new poetry to have different ideas about itself, sometimes pointing in the direction of semantic investigation, as in the poetry of the Syrian poet Ali Ahmad Sa'ad, who has taken the pen name 'Adonis' and has been influenced by European, and especially French, ideas, sometimes being more explicitly political and capable of rousing large audiences, as in early works by the Palestinian Mahmoud Darwish or the Syrian Nizar Qabbani. New poems by the latter two poets, often coming after major public events, have been greeted in the Arab world as events in themselves.

All this is a far cry from poetry considered as a form of linguistic ingenuity, or poetry as a form of aristocratic entertainment, with the poet acting as an ornament of the patron's circle.

While we do not have space here to look in detail at the Arabic poetry of the 1950s and 1960s, anyone wanting guidance should perhaps be familiar with the work of certain 'canonical' modern Arab poets.[27] Al-Sayyab would certainly be one of these, having fashioned what one critic calls a poetry of 'myth and ... archetype' that suggests, something as Eliot had done in *The Waste Land*, that rebirth could only come from the 'aridity of Arab life' in a way 'analogous to the falling of rain over a parched land'. It is to poems such as 'In the Arab Maghreb', written at the time of the Algerian war of independence in the 1950s, that 'al-Sayyab owes his fame and supremacy in modern Arabic poetry,' as well as to perhaps his best-known poem, 'Song of the Rain'. Al-Sayyab's compatriots, al-Malai'ka and al-Bayati, are also securely in the canon, the latter sounding much like Ezra Pound in calling for the 'crushing' of 'Romantic sentimentality, Classical rigidity, oratorical poetry and the literature of ivory towers' and the fashioning of a radically new poetry.[28]

From the Lebanese group and mostly Levantine poets publishing in the *Shi'r* and *al-Adab* reviews, Adonis calls for special mention. This poet, impossible to summarize, sees poetry as 'a challenge to logic ... a change in the order of things, a rebellion against traditional forms and the poetic order', pointing to the influence on him of French ideas of the *poète maudite* and the poet's 'revolutionary' role, at least with regard to language. Adonis has set out his ideas in essay form, for example in his *Introduction to Arab Poetics*,[29] which argues for a 'modernism' in Arabic poetry that looks both to classical Arab models and to modern European, especially French, poetry. It imagines modern Arabic poetry as being in a state of permanent revolt against 'traditionalist mentality'. A rather different poet, less obviously associated with the manifestos coming

Your eyes are a forest of palms at dusk.

Or two balconies before the moon's departure.

When your eyes smile the vines bring forth leaves,

And the lights dance like the moon on the river,

Trembling under the oars, softly in the dusk,

As if stars are glittering in the depths ...

And then sink in a cloud of transparent sorrow

Like the sea open-handed, cloaked by night,

With winter warmth and autumn's trembling;

Like birth and death, darkness and light.

My soul wakes to a tremulous weeping,

A wild rapture embracing the sky,

Like a child's ecstacy when he fears the moon,

As if the arches of clouds drink in the mist

And drop by drop it melts into rain.

The children shouting in the vineyards

And the stillness of sparrows in the trees tickled by

The rainsong ...

Rain

Rain

Rain.

عيناكِ غابتا نخيلٍ ساعة السحر
أو شرفتان راحَ ينأى عنهُما القمر
عيناكِ حين تبسمان تُورقُ الكروم
وترقصُ الأضواءُ .. كالأقمار في نهر
يرجُّهُ المجدافُ وَهْنًا ساعة السحر ...
كأنّما تنبضُ في غوريهما النجوم

وتغرقان في ضبابٍ من أسىً شفيف
كالبحر سرَّحَ اليدين فوقهُ المساء
دفءُ الشتاء فيه و ارتعاشةُ الخريف
و الموتُ و الميلادُ و الظلامُ و الضياء
فتستفيقُ ملء روحي، رعشةُ البكاء
ونشوةٌ وحشية تعانق السماء
كنشوةِ الطفلِ إذا خاف من القمر

كأنَّ أقواسَ السحابِ تشربُ الغيوم ...
وقطرةً فقطرةً تذوبُ في المطر ...
وكركرَ الأطفالُ في عرائش الكروم
ودغدغت صمتَ العصافير على الشجر
أنشودةُ المطر
مطر
مطر
مطر

10. From Iraqi poet Badr Shakir al-Sayyab's poem 'Song of the Rain',
     translated by Mursi Saad El-Din

11.   The Syrian poet Adonis, one of the last century's great experimentalists

out of Beirut, is Qabbani (d. 1998), a poet who did more than most to bring the language of poetry close to the standard language, perhaps accounting for the popularity of his lyric poems and political pieces like 'Footnotes to the Book of Defeat', written in the wake of the 1967 war with Israel, and 'When will the Death of the Arabs be Announced?', a response to the 1993 Oslo Accords between Israel and the Palestinians. There are also Mahmoud Darwish and the Palestinian poets, whose work is discussed in Chapter 4.[30]

Naturally, there are far more poets than these in the post-war canon, even for the restricted period considered here. Egyptian readers, for example, brought up on the works of Egyptian poets in both the classical and colloquial languages, such as Salah Abd al-Sabur, Ahmad Abd al-Mu'ti Hegazi and Amal Dunqul writing in the former, and Salah Jahine, Fu'ad Haddad, Ahmad Fu'ad Nigm and Abd al-Rahman al-Abnoudi in the latter, might be surprised to read one critic's estimate[31] that despite its 'long critical experience' the country failed to 'produce ... a poet great enough to utilize all the knowledge gained', unlike in the 'poetic stronghold' of Iraq.

In poetry, as in politics, there has long been a rivalry for leadership in the Arab world.

Occupation and Diaspora:
the Literature of Modern Palestine

Modern Palestine has given rise to a literature that is in some respects unique in the Arab world, and Palestinian writers and intellectuals have enjoyed an influence in Arab letters out of all proportion to the country's size, matching the role that Palestine and the Israeli-Palestinian conflict have played in Arab affairs since the end of the Second World War. That much at least, lifted from the introduction to this book, is well known and relatively uncontroversial. However, the fact that modern Palestinian literature is in the main not politically propagandistic can be surprising to those who do not know it well. While Palestinian literature cannot help but be politically aware, its relation to politics is usually oblique.

Palestinian writers have tended to stand back from what has seemed to be the permanent state of crisis that has enveloped their country since at least the declaration of the state of Israel in 1948, mostly choosing to address the human consequences of this situation. They have emphasized the suffering that this crisis has brought to individuals from every walk of life, sometimes employing a black sense of humour to do so. They have also explored what it might mean to be identified as a 'Palestinian writer,' particularly when Palestinians have long been divided between those living 'within', whether in the Occupied Territories or in Israel proper, and those living 'without', in the Arab countries or further afield. Should Palestinian writers write about Palestine at the expense of everything else, aiming to serve as 'spokesmen' for the people from whom they come? Or should they have the same kind of loyalties as any other kind of literary writer, first and foremost to their writing? Questions of this sort are explored in this chapter, which gives an overview of main themes in modern Palestinian literature, including Palestinian historical experience, the fact of dispossession and exile, and the possibility of return.

The declaration of the state of Israel in May 1948 divided the British mandate territory of Palestine into three parts. There was, first of all, the part of it that became Israel, and most of the Palestinian refugees forced out by the violence that accompanied the declaration came from here. An estimated three quarters of a million of them poured into camps in neighbouring countries such as Lebanon, or into those parts of the former mandate territory that were ceded either to Jordan or to Egypt, the West Bank and the Gaza Strip, respectively. These areas now made up the second and third parts of what had until then been one Arab country. The experience of 1948 and its after-effects, whether in the bitterness of dispossession and exile or in the new problems that arose for the Arab citizens of the new state of Israel, henceforth became leading themes for generations of Palestinian writers.[1]

One of the best-known of these is Ghassan Kanafani, a writer, journalist and political activist who was himself caught up in the 1948 exodus from Palestine. Like many others in similar circumstances Kanafani lived an unstable life, living and working by turns in Syria, Kuwait and Lebanon and finally becoming a spokesman for the

Popular Front for the Liberation of Palestine, one of the political factions that emerged in the 1960s. He was assassinated in Beirut in 1972. Kanafani's literary work, collected in various volumes of short stories published in the 1960s and several novels, captures Palestinian life in exile in the decades after 1948, notably in the novellas *Men in the Sun* and *All That's Left to You*.[2]

Men in the Sun is Kanafani's best-known work, and it is probably also one of the best-known pieces of modern Palestinian literature. In it, he describes the attempt of four Palestinians to cross the border from Iraq into neighbouring Kuwait in search of work. The latter country, experiencing an economic boom as a result of oil, is in need of cheap labour. However, the Palestinians, being stateless, do not have the necessary entry papers, and they are forced to fall back on one of the human traffickers that ply the desert roads between the two countries. 'A man can collect money in the twinkling of an eye in Kuwait,' one of the four assures himself, having first made the long desert crossing from Jordan to Iraq and now waiting to be smuggled across the border into Kuwait. Before he can collect that money, however, he must make the crossing, and as is often the case with such operations, extortion, or worse, is the norm. There are horrifying stories of Palestinians being abandoned in the desert by unscrupulous traffickers, who leave them to die under the baking sun.

The four eventually meet a lorry driver who agrees to take them across the border in exchange for five dinars, considerably less than the standard fee. The plan is for them to hide in the lorry's tank as it crosses the border (it is a water-tanker), re-emerging from the stifling heat inside once safely past the border controls. All goes well until the driver is held up at a border post, and his human cargo suffocate before he is able to release them. As he drives around the outskirts of Kuwait City looking for somewhere to dump the bodies a question comes to his mind: 'why didn't you knock on the sides of the tank? Why didn't you bang on the sides of the tank? Why? Why? Why?'

Men in the Sun presents the plight of Palestinians unable to find work in the sometimes appalling conditions of the refugee camps, or, legally, elsewhere. *All That's Left to You* presents a variation on this theme, 'what is left' to the characters in this story being either poverty as refugees in the Gaza Strip, or death while trying to cross into Jordan. Like *Men in the Sun*, the story employs several narrators, and it is told from multiple points of view, including that of the surrounding desert. Also like *Men in the Sun*, it captures the 'balance sheet of remnants, the balance sheet of losses, the balance sheet of death' that lies in wait for Palestinians living as refugees in the camps and overtaken by feelings of frustration and bitterness. This half-life is buoyed up only by thoughts of escape or of return to a homeland that has now itself been absorbed by Israel.

For Hamid, the story's protagonist, sixteen years of living as a refugee in Gaza have brought only bitterness, and he resolves to make the twelve-hour desert crossing to Jordan. For his sister Maryam, life in the camps has brought other pressures, and she feels obliged to give up hopes of a better life and to settle instead for the one she has, deciding to marry Zakaria despite the latter's reputation as a collaborator. Hamid condemns her for this, all that's left for her in his eyes being shame. 'The slut couldn't wait,' he comments. 'She came to me with a child throbbing in the womb. And the father? That dog Zakaria.' One interesting feature of this story is its focus on a woman's frustration, and not just a man's, and this is told through the ebbing away, over time, of a young woman's hopes of marriage. 'Every morning, as I changed,' Maryam reflects, 'the clock would sound its melancholy chime.' Marriage to Zakaria seems to offer her some hope of a future, since there is no other form of escape.

Kanafani's work deals with the lives of Palestinian refugees in the decades after 1948, presenting an account of the results of dispossession and exile. Another writer presenting this experience is Emile Habiby, though his work is very different from Kanafani's, and it is possibly unique in its focus on the Arab citizens of Israel rather than on the Palestinian refugees. These people, the 'Israeli Arabs', are composed of Palestinians who remained within the borders of Israel after that state's declaration. Habiby, born in 1922, was himself a leading member of them, becoming both a well-known journalist (editor of *El-Itchad* from 1972 to 1989) and a member of the Israeli Knesset (1951–1972 Communist Party List). His best-known work, the strangely titled *Secret Life of Saeed the 'Pessoptimist*,[3] mixes pessimism with optimism about the Israeli Arabs' situation, hence the novel's title. So bizarre can this situation seem that Saeed, the novel's narrator and protagonist, scarcely knows whether to laugh or cry.

Written in short sections, the book purports to be the story of Saeed's life, beginning with his 'claim to have met creatures from outer space' and a 'report [that] his life in Israel was all due to the munificence of an ass'. Yet, though employing a form of black humour for which Habiby became famous, the book touches on serious themes, such as the persistence of Palestinian memory despite attempts to uproot it and the connections between Palestinian history and the wider history of the Arabs. Indeed, Palestine, Habiby emphasizes, is not just a Palestinian concern. It is also an Arab one, and its history is a part of that of the wider Arab world. 'Take Acre, for example,' Saeed's teacher instructs him. This 'is not a new city' but instead is one that has a long history behind it, which, until recently, was part of the history of the Arabs. In the medieval period the city often changed hands – when the Crusaders conquered it, for example, or when it was liberated by Saladin after the battle of Hittin (1187) – and it has continued to do so up until the present. However, the important thing, Saeed's teacher tells him, is not the fact that Acre, like the rest of the region, has a colourful history of conquest and counter-conquest behind it, but rather that the conquerors, whoever they may be, tend to 'consider as true history only what they have themselves fabricated.' This entails a need to put together an alternative history, which is that of the conquered. While Palestinian villages in Israel have been demolished or renamed in an attempt to deny the Arab history of the area, this does not mean that the memory of them has been lost. On the contrary, memory – history – returns under the most unlikely circumstances, as it does in Saeed's narrative when people vie with each other to give the names of their obliterated villages. 'Please do not expect me, my dear sir, after all this time, to remember the names of all the villages laid waste to which these figures made claim,' says Saeed ironically, having just listed them. 'We of Haifa used to know more about the villages of Scotland than we did about those of Galilee,' used, that is, until they are reminded of them in Habiby's novel.

Saeed refers to a form of storytelling he calls the 'oriental imagination', which connects to the habit of mind identified as 'pessoptimism'. Isn't this, he asks, what makes life for the Arabs in Israel possible? 'Had it not been for their "oriental imagination", would those Arabs of yours, my dear sir, have been able to live a single day in this country?' he asks, giving the example of an Arab youth who, slamming into another car in traffic in Tel Aviv, screams out that the other driver is an Arab and thereby saves himself from the crowd's hostility. 'Wasn't it his oriental imagination that saved him?' There are other examples. 'Shlomo works in one of Tel Aviv's best hotels. Isn't he really Sulaiman, son of Munirah, from our own quarter?'; '"Dudi", isn't he really Mahmud?' How could these people 'earn a living in a hotel, restaurant, or filling station without help from their oriental imagination,' asks Saeed, pointing to the 'pess-optimistic' strategies resorted to by Palestinians in their attempts to get by as Arab citizens of Israel. Nevertheless, though often successful these strategies do not always work, and in one of the best-known instances of Habiby's mordant humour Saeed describes how 'a flag of surrender, flying on a broomstick, becomes a banner of revolt.' Having heard instructions on Radio Israel during the 1967 war that the Arabs are to raise white flags in surrender, Saeed raises his white flag even though he lives in Haifa in the heart of Israel. 'You can't have too much of a good thing,' he says. But on this occasion he is betrayed by his 'oriental imagination'. Raising a white flag under these circumstances is seen 'as an indication that you regard Haifa as an occupied city and are therefore advocating its separation from the state'!

Much Palestinian literature captures the texture of Palestinian experience, whether in the refugee camps or as part of the diaspora, as in works by Kanafani, or within Israel itself, as in Habiby's *Saeed the Pessoptimist*. Both sets of material make sometimes bitter criticisms of the treatment the Palestinians have received at the hands of the Arab states, as much as they have at those of Israel.[4] They also make criticisms of Palestinian society more generally.

In his novels published in the 1960s, for example, the Syrian-American writer and academic Halim Barakat takes aim at Palestinian society as well as at Israel. His *Six Days*, originally published in 1961,[5] describes the siege of a fictional city, Dayr Albahr, and suggests that 'the enemy is not the only problem,' for 'our enemy is inside as well' in the shape of traditionalist attitudes. The characters in this novel explore their options against a background of military threat and stale political rhetoric. Fareed, for instance, is frustrated, wanting 'to rip the veils from the women, stab the men's bloated stomachs, slap the constant smiling, oblivious faces, and spit on those who sell their property and run.' He is tempted to emigrate to the West, or to go to the Gulf where money can be made, leaving behind 'the rabble, the great traditions, the narrow streets, the veiled women, and the walled-off houses' that for him are Palestine. Similarly Lamya, a young woman fed up with being treated like a 'submissive lamb' and with men who are 'not interested in a woman except as an object to sleep with', dreams of London, which for her represents personal freedom. Only Suhail decides to stay, though his decision is not made easily. On the contrary, 'whatever made him think he could abandon his culture,' he asks himself. The truth is 'he cannot escape it' much as a part of him at least might wish to do so.

A later novel, *Days of Dust*, continues Barakat's dissection of Palestinian society, this time in the context of the 1967 war.[6] The war resulted in Arab defeat and in the occupation by Israel of the West Bank, Gaza Strip and Golan Heights, as well as of the Sinai Peninsula until the Camp David Accords in the late 1970s. The novel is divided into six sections that reflect its six-day course, the first section capturing the atmosphere of 'hope mixed with ... profound fear' that reigned in Arab capitals immediately before war broke out and criticizing what the narrator sees as the 'underdeveloped and uncoordinated' character of the Arab world, 'living in the twentieth century only in outward appearance' and given to vain and empty gestures. Even the political upheavals that had helped to modernize Arab societies in the 1950s, the narrator feels, were mere 'revolts, not social revolutions'. These reflections on Arab society, part of the discourse of the time, swiftly give way to the reality of the war itself, which is seen from perspectives in Jericho, the West Bank, Jerusalem and Beirut, where Ramzy, the main narrator, lives. The novel criticizes the Israeli forces, as well as what is seen as the unquestioning support the West has given to Israel. At the end of the war, for example, the narrator comments on the 'Zionists and their friends ... jumping for joy in the streets of New York City.'

Nevertheless, the novel also makes bitter criticisms of Arab society. 'We must reject the entire existing structure,' Ramzy says. 'All the "movements" that have arisen are in fact reactionary. They make no attempt to change our inherited customs and institutions,' which the war has demonstrated must be changed. He wants 'to destroy [his country's] institutions and organizations, its fable-filled, otherworldly constitution imported without modification from days gone by.' These hopes of change, however, are frustrated, and at the war's end there are yet more Palestinian refugees, their lives now 'the property of governments, organizations, [and] associations'. Whereas before the war Ramzy 'had not been able to visit Haifa or Jaffa or Acre or Safad or Nazareth or Ramla or Lydda', since these originally Arab towns were located after 1948 in Israel, following Israel's 1967 occupation of the West Bank he is not able to visit 'Jerusalem or Ramallah or Bethlehem or Hebron or Nablus or Jenin or Qalqilya or Tulkarum' either, all of which are Palestinian towns and cities under Israeli military occupation.

Barakat's work suggests that the failure of Palestinian and Arab society to modernize has left it open to attack. Other, mostly less polemical, representations of that society can be found in the work of Palestinian writers who have written personal testimonies, such as *A Mountainous Journey* by the poet Fadwa Tuqan, or *The First Well* by the novelist, poet and critic Jabra Ibrahim Jabra.

A Mountainous Journey portrays 'the struggle, deprivation and enormous difficulties' faced by a woman growing up in traditional Palestinian society.[7] Born in Nablus on the West Bank in 1917, Tuqan was her mother's seventh child, and her father, wanting a son, dated his daughter's birth by the death of a male cousin. Her whole childhood, she says, was marked by 'the social restraint and subjugation imposed on women' in traditional society, blighting her emotional and intellectual development. Her mother's distance from her children, her 'hidden unhappiness' was, Tuqan believes, the result of her never having had 'the right to express her feelings or her views'. Later, when Tuqan herself withdraws into thoughts of self-harm and suicide, her mother is 'unable to save me ... her individuality [having] been so debilitated by subjugation.' While Tuqan went on to become one of Palestine's best-known poets, known for her commitment to the nationalist cause, the experiences of her early life seem never to have left her, her male relatives, with the exception of her brother Ibrahim (himself a well-known poet), apparently doing everything possible to frustrate her education. They represented 'in the most flagrant manner possible the rigidity of the Arab male and his absolute inability to maintain a personality that was healthy and whole.'

Tuqan suggests that many of these traditionalist attitudes were broken by the events of 1948. Indeed, 'when the roof fell in on Palestine, the veil fell off the face of the Nablus women.' Previously, a woman, even a member of the elite, 'was at the mercy of her brother, even if he was unemployed and no use to himself' or others. Her options outside the household were limited, and as for marriage, 'it was either [to] a paternal cousin or virginity to the grave.' Like the male members of her family, Tuqan was horrified by the 'devilish British intrigue' that led to her country's break-up. Yet, when she came to write about such things she found it impossible to 'compose political poetry', since, as a woman, she was 'shut up inside these walls' and could not 'participate in the turmoil of life outside'. These things began to change in the 1950s, when what Tuqan calls the 'traditional structure of Arab society' was shaken to the core, allowing new roles for women to emerge. Nevertheless, Tuqan was still an exception as far as Palestinian women were concerned, making her autobiography a remarkable document from the period.[8]

Another view of what it was like to grow up in Palestine before 1948 is given in the first part of Jabra Ibrahim Jabra's autobiography, *The First Well*.[9] Jabra, who died in 1994, has a reputation as a writers' writer, and his novels, among them *The Ship* and *The Search for Walid Masoud*, are an acquired taste. The latter work,[10] for example, retells modern Palestinian history through a search for the eponymous Masoud carried out by Dr Jawad Husni, a friend. Masoud has disappeared while driving to Syria from Baghdad, leaving his car and a recorded tape, the contents of which are unclear. The search for him becomes an opportunity to reconstruct the meaning of his life. As Husni puts it, it is part of 'an abstract intellectual search for the rejuvenation of the Arab nation, and, with that peculiarly Palestinian zeal, to examine the entire Arab way of life on every level.' While the flair and narrative experiment of Jabra's novel are everywhere apparent, such an 'abstract intellectual search' may not appeal in translation. The novel's conclusion is that Masoud was 'the product of his life, and the lives of those around him, the product of his own particular time and of our time in general, all at once.'

Jabra's autobiographical writings, on the other hand, have great charm, and they help to explain the high reputation he enjoys in modern Arab letters. Born in Bethlehem in 1920, he was educated in Jerusalem and England, and he made frequent scholarly trips abroad, notably to the United States. He left Palestine in 1948 and lived for the rest of his life in Baghdad. He is the co-author of a novel, *World Without Maps*, written with Saudi novelist Abdelrahman Munif, and of a well-received account of modern Iraqi art. In *The First Well* Jabra gives an account of his boyhood in Bethlehem, writing of 'the events of early childhood' – the memoir halts with the family's 1932 move to Jerusalem – 'that reach us as a sort of mix of memories and dreams'. These things are the contents of 'the first well' of early childhood, to which in later life one may be tempted to return. In Jabra's case, the 'well' contains his schooldays, his family's early poverty and his memories of the religious life of Bethlehem, at the time a small town of just a few thousand inhabitants. He writes enchantingly of Christmas in Bethlehem and of the festivities that took place at the Church of the Nativity in honour of the Greek Orthodox Patriarch, arriving from Jerusalem at the head of an immense procession. Easter was a time of flowers, and, in the afternoons, of 'flocks of swallows that filled the azure air'. Looking out of his schoolroom windows, Jabra could see the 'domes of the Church of the Nativity, and, beyond them, the surrounding hills'.

In a later volume of memoirs, *Princesses' Street*, his last book,[11] Jabra turns to his life as a student in England and his adult life in Baghdad, particularly in the early 1950s when the city was experiencing a 'golden age with its creative aspirations and eagerness for change'.

Jabra was caught up in that excitement, and he includes some fascinating vignettes from the period. These include an encounter with Agatha Christie, in Baghdad with her husband the archaeologist Max Mallowan, who was excavating at the time at Nimrud. Christie, like Mrs Ramsay in Woolf's novel *To the Lighthouse*, spends her time knitting as her husband's conversation swirls about her. Apparently, Jabra comments, she was 'the only person in the room who was not suffering from the fever of writing and did not know its agonies and pains.' There is much surprise when he discovers that 'Mrs Mallowan' is the author of novels that 'I had read since my youth ... [and that are] the delightful and exciting intellectual recreation for millions of people.' (Christie is a popular author in the Arab world.)

However, more important than his encounter with Christie are Jabra's reflections on Baghdad in the politically charged decade of the 1950s, the publication of his first work in Beirut, and his comments on the intellectual atmosphere of the time. In Baghdad 'there were young women itching for their freedom ... there were poets and short-story writers seeking to create new forms in everything they wrote. There were painters ... [and] persons specializing in economic, social, political, philosophical, and historical thought ... announcing the good news of a forthcoming modernity that would change the whole Arab world.' This was all part of the sense of the 'wonderful beginning' that overtook the region in the 1950s with the crumbling of European colonialism. In the Iraqi case things soon began to go disastrously wrong.

The memoirs by Jabra and Tuqan contain testimony from the decades before and after 1948. More recent memoirs, such as the Palestinian poet Mourid Barghouti's *I Saw Ramallah*, focus on the meaning of Palestine for generations that, having spent most of their lives abroad, have only distant memories of the country, if they have first-hand memories of it at all. It also raises the question of 'return', indicating that this is not a simple matter and not only because of the many obstacles that currently prevent it.[12] Will the country answer to the hopes invested in it? Will the returnee, after years spent abroad, be able to find a home there? Such questions are explored in Barghouti's account of his return to Ramallah after a life spent abroad, as they are in novels such as Sahar Khalifeh's *Wild Thorns*.[13]

The latter work appeared in Arabic some ten years into the Israeli occupation of the West Bank and long before the Palestinian uprising, or *intifada*, that began against Israeli rule in the late 1980s.[14] The novel begins with the narrator, Usama al-Karmi, returning from Jordan to the Occupied Territories. There is the usual brutality at the border, but what awaits him on the other side is not what he expected. True, there is the daily humiliation of occupation, reflected in the poor wages and few social protections afforded to Palestinian workers compared with their Israeli counterparts. However, there is also an apparent indifference on the part of the Palestinians 'inside' to the tide of political rhetoric reaching them from their compatriots 'outside' and from the surrounding Arab countries. It is easy, one character explains, for those abroad to urge resistance to the occupation, instructing those within to 'bear all the burdens of risk and sacrifice' when they do not themselves live in Palestine and have possibly never visited it. 'Israeli cash is better than starvation', and Palestinian workers in Israeli factories 'stick up two fingers ... when they hear all that pompous talk of "inter-Arab aid for Palestine"', preferring to get on with life 'while the radio goes on spewing out songs of hope and fervour.'

The Israeli occupation is presented as having 'corrupted' Palestinian society in the Occupied Territories, distorting the economy by bringing in benefits unseen under Jordanian rule. It has also broken the rigid class structure that prevailed before 1948 in particular, attacked by writers such as Barakat and Tuqan. Israel's occupation has brought money and employment to Palestinians who were previously tenant farmers. They did not own the land, and, that being so, one elderly farmer asks, 'why should we care about it? Why should we die for it?' It is sentimentality to suppose that it was ever really theirs. Khalifeh's novel, like others before and after it, criticizes the Palestinian elites as well as the Israelis. 'Who's responsible for the country's lack of industrialization? Who's to blame for the backwardness of the workers?' the narrator's associates ask. The novel ends, like those by Barakat, on hopes of social reconstruction.

Complications attendant on return are also explored in Barghouti's prize-winning memoir *I Saw Ramallah*.[15] This records the author's return to his hometown of Ramallah on the West Bank after some three decades in exile. Crossing the River Jordan, Barghouti remembers the last time he made this journey, in the other direction, immediately before the 1967 war: making it now, he meditates on his return to a homeland in which he cannot help but feel a stranger and on his return to a past that he has outgrown. Such thoughts give way to a narrative, an 'existential account of displacement' according to Edward Said in his foreword, that mixes recognition with disappointment and views adult life through the lens of student hopes held thirty years before. Visiting Dar Ra'd, one of seven neighbouring villages that are home to his extended family, Barghouti looks in on 'the room [in which] I was born four years before the birth of the state of Israel'. Outside, this village, like the settlements around it, has been marked by a lifetime's events and by the facts of occupation and diaspora. 'I greeted the neighbours, and I recognized none of them ... Husbands, sons, and daughters have been distributed among graves and detention camps, jobs and parties and factions of the Resistance, the lists of martyrs, the universities, the sources of livelihood in countries near and far ... Calgary to Amman, Sao Paolo to Jeddah, Cairo to San Francisco, Alaska to Siberia.' That being so, what might it mean to return to a homeland that has changed almost beyond recognition? How to deal with the fact that one has oneself changed? Whatever the answers for others may be, for himself

Barghouti suggests that life, a set of 'temporary permanencies', 'will not be simplified'. Palestine is not the promised land. The 'homeland [is not] the medicine for all sorrows.'

Nevertheless, though a life spent looking back on a lost homeland cannot be a satisfying one, trying to forget that homeland, or never having had it, are not solutions either. Barghouti reflects on the experience of Palestinians, born in exile, who have no memories of home. While his own memories may be distorted, and a habit of looking back on loss may have 'forced us to remain with the old' at the expense of the new, at least he has memories of a childhood home, a 'first well' in Jabra's terms, to which in adult life he can return. Israel, on the other hand, 'has created generations without a place whose colours, smells, and sounds they can remember: a first place that belongs to them, that they can return to in their memories in their cobbled-together exiles.' The occupation of the West Bank in particular 'has created generations of us that have to adore an unknown beloved: distant, difficult, surrounded by guards, by walls, by nuclear missiles, by sheer terror.'

Finally, no account of modern Palestinian literature would be complete without mention of Palestine's poets, at least one of whom, Mahmoud Darwish, has an international reputation. While modern Palestinian poetry can scarcely be understood without reference to modern Arabic poetry more generally, its specific feature is its 'Palestinian' character. This can lead to a temptation for Palestinian poets to write about Palestine at the expense of everything else, or to present themselves as 'spokesmen' for the people from whom they come.

Darwish himself has perhaps not been immune from this temptation, the danger of which is that it can lead to poetry drawing on stock motifs. In the Palestinian case the dangers of political 'platform poetry' are acute, and they are referred to by Barghouti in *I Saw*

12. Mahmoud Darwish, national poet of Palestine

Ramallah. While Palestinians can scarcely ignore politics, he says, this does not 'justify the overt political approach of Palestinian poetry, in the homeland or the Diaspora. Comedy is also necessary ... Our tragedy cannot produce only tragic writing. We are also living in a time of historical and geographical farce.' This was also Habiby's insight, and it led him to write *Saeed the Pessoptimist.* However, Barghouti goes on to suggest that 'the political approach', if this is understood to mean writing only about politics, or, worse, being close to politicians, is all the more dangerous for poets in that poetry naturally entails 'displacement'. The poet strives 'to escape the dominant language to a language that speaks itself for the first time', which can mean writing about almost anything but a narrow conception of politics.

In his best work Darwish has explored similar issues. Born in 1941 in a village in Galilee, he and his family were forced into exile in 1948, and he has lived since in various Arab capitals, including Cairo and Beirut. He has been the editor of an important literary review, *al-Karmel.* Darwish's poetry can be read in various English translations,[16] and it contains textbook examples of poems of Palestinian loss and exile, pieces such as 'We Travel Like Other People' ('We travel like other people, but we return to nowhere') or 'Athens Airport' ('Athens Airport changes its people every day. But we have stayed put ... waiting for the sea') from the 1986 collection *Fewer Roses,* capturing such experience. However, his work also contains material that attempts larger reflections, including an ambitious memoir, *Memory for Forgetfulness*, written after the 1982 Israeli invasion of Beirut.[17]

This book, a long work of 'prose poetry', connects the author's experience of being trapped in his flat in war-torn Beirut to the fate of the Palestinian refugees around him, who, deprived of work and equal rights in their host country of Lebanon, are seen as the problem, 'making trouble, violating the rules of hospitality', and now allegedly responsible for the war. 'Why don't you go back to your own country?' he is asked. Israel will then have less reason to invade. Making coffee in his flat, walking through the streets, visiting friends as the bombs rain down, what, Darwish asks, is the role of the Palestinian poet under such circumstances? 'Palestine has been transformed from a birthplace to a slogan', and one that all too often does not even serve the Palestinians' interests, now that Beirut, 'birthplace for thousands of Palestinians who know no other cradle', is being evacuated under the impact of Israeli bombs. 'No one wants to forget. More accurately, no one wants to be forgotten', he writes, and as a result he chooses to 'join battle', in his translator's words, 'against oblivion', producing a memory for forgetfulness that is 'not chronicle, journey, history, memoir, fiction, myth, or allegory, but all of them together'.

Darwish's work can be understood as an act of memory and a set of meditations on the role and responsibilities of the Palestinian poet. But he himself has been ambivalent about that role, and he has criticized his earlier poems for being too direct, too crude, insufficiently poetic and too rhetorical. Darwish, in fact, is a man of enormous literary culture, and he has reflected deeply about the relationship between Palestinian poetry and Arabic poetry and between Arabic poetry and world poetry, as well as about his responsibilities to himself, to his audiences and to Palestine. Reading a recent collection of interviews with Darwish, one is reminded strongly of W. B. Yeats, whose developing responsibilities to Ireland similarly lay at the root of much of his poetry.[18] Being the 'Palestinian national poet' is an enormous responsibility calling for a certain distance if one is not to be imprisoned in the role. Less well known, but well worth reading, is Samih al-Qasim, who, born a few years earlier than Darwish (in 1939), nevertheless has not achieved anything like the latter's international reputation. Like Habiby, he has spent his life in Israel. Al-Qasim writes short, pointed lyrics, such as 'Travel Tickets', which perhaps well summarizes the hopes and fears of a whole generation:

> On the day you kill me
> You'll find in my pocket
> Travel tickets
> To peace,
> To the fields and the rain,
> To people's conscience.
> Don't waste the tickets.

Disillusion and Experiment

Shortly after the defeat of the Arab forces in the 1967 Six Day War with Israel, a defeat dubbed the *Naksah* ('setback') in Arabic and ushering in a period of sometimes agonized self-reflection, Naguib Mahfouz published a collection of short stories entitled *At the Bus Stop*. The title story sets the tone. A group of people are waiting for a bus in Cairo, when bizarre, and increasingly violent, events start to take place around them. Are these events being staged as part of a film, and, if so, where are the cameras and the director? A thief runs past; there is a car crash; a herd of camels and a group of tourists pass by, like images taken from a dream, or from a spectacle that is taking place without reference to those watching it. When the people at the bus stop ask the police to intervene, the police turn their guns on them and shoot them.[1]

The story might be taken as a bleak verdict on events in the Arab world in the 1960s, but it is by no means alone for that. Regimes across the Arab world had failed to keep their promises with regard either to development goals or to greater democracy and civil liberties. Nasser's Egypt, which had represented wider hopes across the Arab world, had turned into a police state at home, characterized by fear and a personality cult of an egregious kind. Abroad, the Arab world, with the exception of Lebanon and some other countries, had developed a reputation as a region characterized by dictatorship, together with failing development goals and, often, war and poverty. To cap it all, many of the Arab countries had now suffered a disastrous military defeat by Israel, revealing corruption and incompetence on a wide scale. Aside from the bitter reflections of Mahfouz, the work of two Egyptian writers, Sonallah Ibrahim and Gamal al-Ghitany, provide contrasting responses to this situation.

Ibrahim is one of the contemporary Arab world's best-known writers and a prominent representative of the 'generation of the 1960s', in other words of the generation of Arab writers that started to publish in the 1960s or that adopted the label of 'sixties writers'. For one critic, this was the generation that began to see itself in terms of revolt, sixties writers typically considering 'themselves as experimentalists in their own right [and] striking out on their own'.[2] For another, the writers of the generation of the 1960s, including Ibrahim, are concerned to 'parody and satirize power', being engaged in a 'rereading and rewriting of history in which both writer and reader are implicated'.[3] In his first book, *The Smell of It*,[4] the one that made his reputation, Ibrahim uses a quotation from Joyce's *Portrait of the Artist as a Young Man* as his epigraph: 'this race and this country and this life produced me ... and I shall express myself as I am'.

Stephen Dedalus's truculence and independence of mind, as well as his insistence that he, as much as the sundry Irish nationalists, Gaelic revivalists and Roman Catholic reactionaries around him, has the right to represent his country, provide a kind of model for Ibrahim, apparently exasperated, like Joyce's Stephen, by aspects of the society that has formed him. Ibrahim is on record as saying that his aim in this novel was to record 'reality as it is, without any attempt at interpretation or commentary ... simply to record without concern [either] for social conventions ... [or] for literary conventions.' Like Joyce, he experienced problems with the authorities as a result, the complete text of *The Smell of It* only appearing in Arabic in 1986, some twenty years after the publication of the original, bowdlerized edition and long after the appearance of the English translation.[5]

Born in Cairo in 1937, Ibrahim became a writer and political activist at an early age, and he was arrested by the Nasser regime in 1959 and kept in detention until 1964. Since then he has committed himself to writing. In *The Smell of It* the anonymous narrator recounts the mundane events of his life following his release from prison in a stripped-down prose that has been deliberately voided of affect. He gets up; he reads the papers; he buys some household items and takes the tram into the city centre; he tries to write; he smokes a cigarette; and he masturbates. Literary writing is a particularly complicated activity. Not only is it something that can only be done in breaks snatched between other things, but there is also the question of what to write about and for whom. Rather like in the stories collected in Joyce's *Dubliners*, the tone of this novel is one of frustration and paralysis, with earlier models of what a writer should be, or what he should write about, appearing as a kind of mockery. 'I seized hold of the pen but was unable to write,' the narrator records. 'I took up one of the magazines. There was an article about literature and the sort of things one should write about. The writer said that Maupassant said that the artist must create a world that is simpler, more beautiful than ours. He said that literature should be optimistic, throbbing with the most beautiful of sensations ... I put my hand down to my thigh and started playing with myself. At last I gave a deep sigh. Tired, I sprawled back in my chair, staring vacantly as the paper in front of me. After a while I got up and ... went to the bathroom.'

Writing as a form of masturbation is a bleak outlook for a professional writer to take, even if it is one that here at least has the virtue of being true to life, unlike the contrasting form attributed to Maupassant.

Ibrahim's writing from the 1960s employs a kind of 'exaggerated realism', 'hyper-realism' it is sometimes called, being concerned to capture the texture of life as for him it really is in all its boredom and sterility. However, in his later works, Ibrahim has embarked on what is in some respects a more positive literary programme, and works such as *The Committee* and *Zaat* [6], though they continue the literary agenda begun so strikingly in *The Smell of It*, are directed as much at suggesting other possible ways of apprehending reality as at simply rendering how it is in all its banal detail.

The Committee, for example, recalls the works of Kafka in its presentation of an individual, a writer, who is confronted by an omniscient state that only reveals itself from time to time and then only in the form of a 'Committee' made up of eminent personalities. Following an initial investigation, the Committee's members ask the narrator of this novel to identify something that embodies 'the notable and timeless concepts of this century's civilization'. He answers 'Coca-Cola'. Not only has this product managed to assert itself on a global scale, he explains, 'transforming workers into machines, consumers into numbers, and countries into markets', but it has also exerted considerable political influence. Having explained the influence this product has been able to exert in the 'greatest and richest country in the world' (the USA), the narrator asks the Committee to 'imagine how dominant it is in third world countries, especially in our poor little country' (Egypt).

Unimpressed, the Committee commissions the narrator to produce a work on the 'greatest contemporary Arab luminary'. This commission, dreaded at first, turns out to be unexpectedly interesting, and it begins to absorb the narrator's attention. In particular, it helps him identify the ways in which the apparently unconnected phenomena around him are in fact connected at a deeper level, often seeming to converge on the mysterious figure of 'the Doctor', who is the subject of the narrator's research. Rather like the ubiquitous figure of Zelig invented by Woody Allen in his 1983 film of the same name, the Doctor turns out to be both at the centre of events and marginal to them, appearing at the edges of official photographs, or in the detail of news reports, but seldom if ever occupying centre stage.[7] Yet, for the narrator the Doctor is the most important Arab personality of the age because, like Coca-Cola, he is the one that best represents it in its larger character as well as in its smaller details.

The question of what form the report should take preoccupies the narrator. Should it be a conventional biography, starting with the Doctor's birth and aiming to reconstruct his career? This would have the disadvantage of missing out the 'hidden relationships and connections among a collection of strange and diverse phenomena' that his research has begun to reveal. 'Even if the Doctor doesn't bake the pie,' one slogan reminds him, 'he's first in line for a slice.' Rather like the case of the narrator's identification of Coca-Cola as the most important representative of the century's civilization, the Doctor's ubiquity is not in question. It is how to make sense of it that exercises the narrator. The Committee asks him how he has managed to find out so much about the Doctor, greeting his answer 'from the newspapers' with incredulous laughter, since the news media serve in this novel as much to conceal reality as to represent it. However, this is in fact the truth, even if the narrator has had to read the newspapers in a particular way, rearranging cuttings from them in order to constellate events differently from the way in which they are presented in the standard reports, and producing collage-like assemblages of events that invite different interpretations from those officially on offer.

Ibrahim has long had an interest in what gets cut out of standard ways of seeing things – possibly because the censor's scissors have so often snipped at his own texts – and writing for him has increasingly become a form of reconstitution, either setting back together what has been snipped apart, or rearranging the way in which events are customarily seen to allow hidden patterns to be perceived. Procedures of this sort have a distinguished pedigree: Brecht, for example, had hoped both to be able to rearrange reality in order to reveal its deeper structure and to encourage an active habit of mind on the part of his audience through his use of 'epic theatre', which also cuts up narrative and imagines different possible interpretations of events.[8] Ibrahim's interest in such procedures, hinted at in *The Committee*, is taken furthest in his later novel *Zaat*. In this novel Ibrahim cuts up and rearranges standard representations of reality by inserting bits and pieces from newspapers into the fictional narrative. He then invites readers to make their own connections between the materials he has assembled and to draw their own conclusions.

Zaat, which means 'self' in Arabic, is an ordinary woman, so ordinary, in fact, that she is positively dull, and the narrator of the novel is not averse to treating her humdrum, mostly uncomprehending life with heavy-handed irony. Yet, like Flaubert's Bouvard and Pécuchet, the petit-bourgeois protagonists of his novel of the same name, Zaat is important for her typicality rather than for anything special about her, even if her name also parodies that of a princess in a classical Arabic epic, *al-ʿAmira zaat al-Himah*. Asking himself where to begin in finding the meaning of such a life, the narrator decides to start at the very beginning, when Zaat emerged, bloody and screaming, from her mother's womb. However, the narrative only really gets underway when Zaat is engaged to be married sometime in the 1960s, in other words at the time when Ibrahim himself began his writing career during the period of officially socialist, state-led development.

Both for Zaat and for her future husband, Abdel-Maguid Hassan Khamees, shortened to less of a mouthful as Maguid, the 1960s seem to offer unprecedented possibilities for people from the developing middle classes. There are new products, new places to live, and new forms of communication to enjoy, notably television, and before her marriage Zaat spends many evenings seated before the latter with her fiancé, carefully chaperoned by her mother. However, even during this period of actual and official optimism ominous warning signs are not in short supply. When Zaat is obliged to get a job, for example, since she has no connections or relatives in high places, she is shunted into a lowly part of the state bureaucracy at one of Cairo's nationalized newspapers, where she works in the 'Department of News Monitoring and Assessment'. Here she is left much to her own devices, since her boss, knowing what is expected of him, simply submits the same reports over and over again, only altering the dates. As one president gives way to another, marked by a change in the official photographs on the office walls, Zaat and her husband's standard of living begins to fall as the country's exploding population starts to overwhelm the city streets, inflation begins to erode salaries, and once gleaming new apartments sink amid the piles of rubbish that no one any longer bothers to collect. Meanwhile, new and exciting consumer goods start to appear on the market, many priced at several times an annual salary, and while the lot of average Egyptians, such as Zaat, declines, huge fortunes start to be made. The streets fill with expensive imported cars, and evidence of conspicuous consumption spills out from the proliferating five-star hotels.

These developments, hardly noticed by Zaat herself, are introduced in the form of cuttings from various Egyptian, Arab and international newspapers and magazines, which are interleaved between the novel's chapters. Following the narrator's description of Zaat's early married life, for example, the reader is presented with a chapter entirely composed of press clippings. Plucking these out of context and rearranging them with others gives these a kind of mordant humour they presumably did not originally possess, a comment from the Cairo daily *al-Akhbar*, for example, 'only a complete recovery of moral standards will pull Egypt out of its economic crisis', appearing with an estimate of the wealth of Esmat El Sadat, a relative of the late president, 'accumulated over 16 years working as a driver,' at 125 million Egyptian pounds (around GBP 12 million at today's values).

Zaat has been widely commented upon, some considering that Ibrahim's aim is to suggest that consumerism, like some other features of modern Arab society, 'encourages passivity', and seeing in the novel criticism of the sort contained in Ibrahim's earlier short stories, such as 'Across Three Beds in the Afternoon'.[9] In this piece, the protagonists spend most of their time sleeping, when they are not watching television. This story, like *Zaat*, suggests the ways in which a political situation that Ibrahim has characterized as a kind of mix of a lack of popular participation with comprador capitalism can be maintained. However that may be, at the very least *Zaat* contains some startling material relating to the scale of corruption in contemporary Egypt and beyond. While one might have doubts about how far this can be made sense of in translation, since the English version, like the Arabic original,[10] gives only minimal details of the clippings provided and does not go very far in identifying the persons concerned, Ibrahim's 'cut-and-paste' technique is a remarkable innovation in the Arabic novel.

In other works not available in English, Ibrahim has continued the literary project announced in the 1960s. In *Beirut, Beirut*, for example, he turns his attention to the Arab publishing industry, the protagonist travelling to Beirut in order to publish a novel that in one way or another offends 'almost all' Arab regimes.[11] This novel allows Ibrahim to comment on the situation of the writer in the Arab world, while also writing about the civil war in Lebanon. While *Beirut, Beirut* is perhaps a writer's novel, or at least a novel about the travails of being a writer, later novels like *Sharaf* and *Amrikanli* return to more familiar territory.[12] In the former, a young man, idling about the streets gazing at consumer goods he cannot afford, is subjected to a sexual assault at the hands of a wealthy foreigner. Ibrahim may want to see in this an indication of the ways in which Arab populations are invited to prostitute themselves, potentially or actually, to foreign capital, though for at least one critic the novel misfires.[13] The latter novel is the story of an Egyptian academic invited to lecture in the United States at the height of the Monica Lewinski crisis. Though the American university environment is uncongenial to him, the atmosphere at his home university in Cairo is little better, with academic careers being made or broken by how closely individuals are able to conform to dominant religious trends. A recent memoir, a kind of pre-history of *The Smell of It*, has also appeared in Cairo under the title 'Voyeurism'.[14] Though Ibrahim's novels have been getting longer and longer, losing some of the directness of *The Smell of It*, he remains an author to watch.

Gamal al-Ghitany is also a prominent member of the generation of the 1960s, but his writing is very different from Ibrahim's. While the latter has adopted an explicitly political stance, al-Ghitany has made his reputation through research into pre-modern Arabic literary materials, and his politics, though deeply felt, are rather more concealed. Al-Ghitany is also a journalist and editor of the weekly *Akhbar al-Adab*, one of the few literary reviews for a general audience available in Arabic, which is published by the Cairo paper *al-Akhbar*. His best-known novel, one of only two titles translated into English from perhaps a dozen or so published works, is *Zayni Barakat*,[15] this text exemplifying its author's wider literary procedures.

Al-Ghitany first came to prominence in the late 1960s, when, like many other writers of his generation, he published material in *Gallery 68*, the literary showcase of the time edited by an editorial committee including the novelist and critic Edwar al-Kharrat. (The latter's work is discussed below.) A first collection of short stories appeared in 1969 entitled *Papers of a Young Man Who Lived One Thousand Years Ago*, among them a story purportedly referring to events in the al-Maqshara prison in Cairo during the medieval period and told in the language of the time.[16] This experiment al-Ghitany then reworked in novel form to produce *Zayni Barakat*, published in Arabic in 1973 and subsequently translated into most European languages. The historical Zayni Barakat ibn Musa held the office of *muhtasib,* or markets inspector, during the final decades of the Mamluk state in Egypt, managing to retain the post after the Ottoman takeover in 1517 and surviving both the country's last Mamluk sultan and its first Ottoman ruler.[17] In the novel, as its translator points out, he is portrayed as 'the quintessential opportunist and sinister manipulator', a kind of power behind the throne whose charismatic influence allows him to outmanoeuvre all rivals. The 'most striking impression' made by the novel's source text, a history by Muhammad ibn Iyas (1448–c.1522), is that Zayni Barakat 'is a survivor'.

Barakat is the leader of a drive to restore moral order reminiscent of Angelo's campaign in Shakespeare's *Measure for Measure*. Like the latter, 'a man whose blood/Is snow broth [... and] who never feels/The wanton stings and motions of the sense,' he is apparently incorruptible, and his success is advertised as due to 'his virtue and integrity, his honesty and righteousness, his strength and firmness, [and] his revered respectability.' Whereas Angelo is a revolting hypocrite, Barakat turns out to be a man for all seasons, and al-Ghitany's narrative method, which mixes reports by a fictional Venetian traveller, Visconti Gianti, with letters, proclamations, and other documents written in the language of the time, adds up to a kind of polyphonic portrait of the man. We shall probably never know whether Shakespeare, writing under the censorship conditions of his time, intended to make some particular point in his portrait of Angelo. Al-Ghitany, however, almost certainly means his readers to be reminded of a particular individual through his portrait of Barakat, as was the case in many other literary subterfuges at the time.[18] This individual, like Barakat, was 'a man of unknown origin, without roots, on whom fortune suddenly smiled and who claimed that he was going to establish justice on earth', and Edward Said spells out the 'correspondence' in his foreword to the English translation: 'al-Ghitani's disenchanted reflections upon the past directly associate Zayni's role with the murky atmosphere of intrigue, conspiracy and multiple schemes that characterized Abdel Nasser's rule in the 1960s,' which nevertheless survived defeat in 1967. Though the parallels are not exact, they are close enough, and Zayni's charismatic control over the population, his populism and his temporary disappearance following news of the defeat of the Sultan's armies by the Ottomans are enough to make the connection with Nasser.

These two paths, 'exaggerated realism' on the one hand, giving way to politically aware experiment and a critical re-functioning of techniques taken from the pre-modern Arab literary heritage on the other, have provided models for many other writers. However, the two trajectories do not exhaust the possibilities available, and other writers have opened up distinct paths for themselves. Edwar al-Kharrat, for example, has looked to Proust for inspiration in works such as *Rama and the Dragon*, *City of Saffron* and *Girls of Alexandria*, published comparatively late in life from the 1980s onwards.[19] He has also produced critical work that acts as a kind of commentary on the kinds of 'new writing' with which he is associated.

Al-Kharrat was born in 1926 in Alexandria, and during his student years he was involved in radical left-wing politics, leading to his imprisonment between 1948 and 1950. Following a career spent in the cultural bureaucracy, he published his first novel, *Rama and the Dragon*, in 1979, going on to publish over a dozen other works in the decades that followed. In his critical writings, al-Kharrat is ambivalent towards the 'committed' literature that became fashionable in the 1950s. In the wake of the work of al-Sharqawi and Idris, discussed in Chapter 3, which marked a new and 'genuine concern for the vast poverty-stricken inarticulate mass of the people' and went hand in hand with the development hopes of the day, there came a 'growing swell of pompous works of literature that dubbed themselves "socialist" and "realist", he says, yet which in fact were crudely rhetorical,' their characters merely stereotypes ('effigies') in the manner familiar from Soviet-style 'socialist realism'. Such work, al-Kharrat thinks, was aesthetically or philosophically naïve, since it took for granted 'that it was possible and even desirable to portray, or reflect, that is, to represent, *the* reality in literature'. As a result, reality and representation became linked together in a vicious circle, such that only what could be described in realist style was considered the legitimate content of literature, and literature, far from suggesting new ways of thinking, merely reflected and endorsed the official version of things.[20]

For al-Kharrat literature should aim at 'widening the scope of "reality"', rather than simply representing how it appears, and it should be engaged in a work of 'constant questioning'. While this may or may not also be an important consideration, the 'new writing' for which he has argued has had an authenticity component in that, he says, 'the Arab literary mind was nurtured on the epic [and] the frankly phantasmagorical,' and the new writing can be understood as drawing on this 'rich heritage ... while reaping the benefits of the modernist achievements of the West.' Debates of this sort about the merits of realism and other forms of writing are familiar to students of earlier modernist experiments in Europe, al-Kharrat's strictures on realism, for example, recapitulating attacks made by modernist intellectuals on the kind of writing favoured by Marxist critics with a penchant for realism, such as Lukács.[21] What is of interest here, however, is not so much the provenance of al-Kharrat's ideas, their 'reaping the benefits of the modernist achievements of the West', as the ways in which such thinking has found its way into the aesthetics of the Arabic novel and his own novels in particular.

He has drawn up a typology of the kinds of 'new writing' he favours, going from a writing that, like some modernist experiments, seeks to convey the 'entire inner life' in the form of a subjectivism similar to 'stream-of-consciousness' writing styles, to a writing that, rather in the manner of the objectivism favoured by Ibrahim, magnifies the 'alienation, or the estrangement of man' from the events around him. There is also what al-Kharrat calls a 'contemporary mythical current' that draws instead on legends or re-functioned historical and pre-modern materials in the different manners of al-Ghitany in *Zayni Barakat* or Salih in *Bandarshah*. Perhaps al-Kharrat's own novels are best understood in terms of the first of these alternatives, since they are typically concerned to convey the 'entire inner life', including the life of memory. *City of Saffron*, for example, a collection of 'Alexandrian texts', is set in the 1930s in Alexandria, and it consists of the boyhood memories of the first-person narrator, Mikha'il, who grew up in the city. Each of the nine 'texts' making up the novel is built around an image – 'Billowing White Clouds' is the picture with which the book begins – and each of these images connects, rather in the manner of the 'involuntary memory' described by Proust, with a whole tissue of past experience. Moreover, Mikha'il's remembered experience might be taken to be linked with that of al-Kharrat: both the narrator of *City of Saffron* and its author went to school and university in Alexandria; both were raised in difficult circumstances following the deaths of their fathers; both were obliged to work to support their studies, Mikha'il in the novel describing work in the British naval depot at Alexandria during the Second World War, when the German army led by Rommel was almost at the city's gates.

Mikha'il sees his past in indulgent terms, and he reflects on 'this obsession of yours – tinged as it is with irony – with that which has perished, which has been effaced'. Perhaps al-Kharrat's aim in the novel is to reconstruct that 'perished' city, the Alexandria of his childhood, in linguistic form, a sort of 'virtual' city of saffron to make up for the real one that time has swept away. If so, then this is a project he continues in another novel, *Girls of Alexandria*, which reproduces the memories of a slightly older Mikha'il, again in nine named sections. According to the English translator of the two books, *City of Saffron* and *Girls of Alexandria* are 'two excursions into a discourse which continues unbroken ... [The text] illustrates the tension between transient surface experience and the unending dream of life which underpins it.' As in the earlier novel, Mikha'il takes an ironic view of his younger self, of the young man who would order 'Marxist and Trotskyite books and periodicals ... direct from the publishers' in Europe and America, having them delivered to a post office address in Manshiya, a district of Alexandria. 'My belief in life then,' he explains, 'was that Revolution could not dispense with aesthetics ...'

As far as 'transient surface experience' is concerned, the later novel records some of the 'most important event[s] in our recent history', but only as these are witnessed by Mikha'il out of the corner of his eye. Once, changing buses in front of the Cecil Hotel, for example, 'I saw the tanks, armoured cars and troop carriers clattering along the Corniche' to Ras al-Tin Palace to arrest the king (in the 1952 Revolution); earlier there had been the 'long black Packard' car 'belonging to the young Prince Muhammad Reza Pahlavi', later Shah of Iran, on his way to marry Princess Fawzia (in 1939); and later there is 'the deep magical voice which had for so long intoxicated millions and filled their breasts with elation ... "lift up your head, brother, for the age of colonialism has passed"' (the voice is that of Nasser bidding farewell to British colonialism).

In concluding this chapter something should be said about developments in poetry and drama. While the free verse of the 1950s and 1960s has been widely translated, non-Arabic-speaking readers have been less well served as far as contemporary poetry is concerned. Only some major trends have been picked out in what follows, together with the work of poets available in translation.

In the 1970s, Arabic poetry entered a period of crisis. Earlier poets such as al-Mala'ika, al-Sayyab and, predominantly, Adonis, had brought about major changes in the forms and language of Arabic poetry, but as a result poetry exhibited a kind of paradox: while on the one hand it had cast off traditional rhetoric in favour of language that was closer to that of educated speech, on the other it had absorbed many of the lessons of European modernist poetry, al-Sayyab borrowing from T. S. Eliot and Edith Sitwell (oddly for English readers) and Adonis finding inspiration in the work of the French surrealists, whose 'revolutionary' poetic programme he adopted. Arabic poetry now sounded more 'modern' and conformed more closely to international norms. However, it also sounded more elitist and more off-putting to ordinary readers. 'A whole generation of poets from Bahrain and Yemen to Morocco sank deeper and deeper into inventiveness for its own sake, unguided by any informed criticism,' writes one critic. By the beginning of the 1980s, 'a large amount of bad poetry had accumulated', some of it marked by experiment for its own sake, some of it loudly attitudinizing in the manner of 'platform poetry'.[22]

Among this material there was nevertheless more modest work, poetry, in other words, that reacted against the grandstanding of the earlier generation by choosing deliberate, anti-heroic deflation. One might think, in British terms, of the puncturing of reputations carried out by the poets associated with 'the Movement' in the 1950s, who were unable to bear what they saw as the posturing of their immediate forebears. The Egyptian poet Salah Abd al-Sabur is an example of a poet who wrote in a more ironical, self-critical tone, the Iraqi Sa'di Yusuf another. One might point, too, to the poetry of the Egyptians Amal Dunqul, Ahmad Abd al-Mu'ti Hegazi and Muhammad Afifi Matar, all of whose work departed in one way or another from what had come before it. The latter has the reputation of being a formidably 'difficult' poet, his work marked by a 'rich intricacy and wonderful strangeness' and 'appealing to connoisseur readers rather than the general Arab public,' in the words of his translators.²³ These poets, like those discussed earlier, write in the 'classical' language, in other words in the Arabic generally used throughout the Arab world for written materials and in formal speech. Yet, the post-war period also saw developments in poetry written in the colloquial, the local Arabic vernacular or dialect, and some of the best-known poets writing in Egypt, for example, have written in the local dialect, though they have not always been recognized by the critics. Such poets include Salah Jahine, Fu'ad Haddad, Ahmad Fu'ad Nigm and Abd al-Rahman al-Abnoudi.

Both Jahine and Haddad began to write in the 1950s, and both looked for inspiration to the vernacular poetry written by the earlier Egyptian poet Bairam al-Tunsi. However, both poets invested their work with aesthetic and political dimensions that poetry in the vernacular had perhaps not previously had: Haddad in particular, of Levantine origin and at home in both French and Arab culture, could hardly be described as 'untutored' despite his choice of the vernacular language, and Jahine used the dialect as a way of mobilizing popular support behind Nasser's policies (which he enthusiastically supported) and finding new audiences for poetry. His best-known work includes the *Ruba'iyyat* (Quatrains) and the 'Songs of the Revolution' in support of the Nasser regime, though he was also a gifted cartoonist.

While Jahine and Haddad died in the 1980s, Nigm and al-Abnoudi, their heirs, are very much alive, and reading them is an invigorating experience for foreign readers, used, perhaps, to a different idea of the poet and of the poet's audience. Both men made their names through performance poetry written in the colloquial language, and their appeal is to an audience that might not have much time for the formal language or difficulty of 'high-brow' poets like Matar. Much of their work has been set to music as songs. Nigm, in particular, became a minor celebrity thanks to his performances of poetry containing often scurrilous satire, these being circulated, *samizdat* fashion, on tape cassette. A performance of work by al-Abnoudi can have an atmosphere more familiar from a sports event than from a poetry reading, which in European countries tend to be sedate, almost apologetic affairs. Nigm has identified himself with the 'ibn al-balad', the perpetual underdog or 'salt of the earth', on whose behalf he claims to speak, and visiting him in the Cairo district of al-Darb al-Ahmar in the 1990s was quite unlike visiting a European poet of comparable fame, or, indeed, like visiting one of Nigm's own fellow poets, for example at their offices at *al-Ahram*. Nigm did not have a telephone, and it was necessary to track his movements from street vendors on the way. He was friendly and affable, though not particularly interested in receiving visitors, especially foreigners with whom communication tends to be limited.[24]

One has the feeling, visiting Nigm or attending one of al-Abnoudi's poetry readings, that theirs is a genuinely popular poetry. There are also traditions of vernacular poetry outside Egypt, for example in Iraq, where one of the best-known vernacular poets is Muzaffar al-Nawwab (b. 1934), who has also written poetry with a directly political content.[25]

Finally, a new generation of poets emerged in the 1990s whose work is also still under-represented in translation. These poets, 'rebels' according to their translator Mohamed Enani, have 'rejected the idea of serious art and [embraced] an eclectic mix of cultural input[s].' They have a marginal position with regard to the cultural establishment, shunning publication in mainstream reviews and setting up independent magazines instead with names like *al-Garad* ('locusts'), *al-Kitaba al-Ukhra* ('alternative writing') and *al-Khitab al-Hamishy* ('marginal discourse'), in which they publish material that marks out new territory in the manner of any avant-garde. Enani's introduction to this material is perhaps more eloquent than any statement by a foreign writer: these poets' 'modes of statement', he says, 'are deliberately anti-Arabic', indicating a desire to break with certain ideas of tradition. Their poems, 'anti-cooperative' and written in a 'private language', can leave their readers at sea.[26] All these qualities are shared with parallel developments in prose writing, as we shall see in the next chapter.

This chapter would not be complete without some account of the drama, which now began to build upon the traditions established by al-Hakim. Whatever other qualities the latter may have had, modesty seems not to have been one of them. He was given, for example, to pointing out that the lack of a tradition of dramatic writing in Arabic presented Arab dramatists with special difficulties, obliging him 'to undertake in thirty years a trip on which the dramatic literature of other languages had spent about two thousand years.'[27] Al-Hakim's play *People of the Cave*, a version of the Qur'anic story of the Sleepers of Ephesus, was greeted on its publication in 1933 as 'the first work in Arabic literature that may be properly called drama' by no less a critic than Taha Hussein, and it bears witness to al-Hakim's determination to make drama into a 'serious branch of literature' and not just a form of entertainment. Yet, while al-Hakim was perhaps almost alone in his endeavours until the 1950s, from this decade on striking developments in drama began to take place across the Arab world, a particularly talented new generation of playwrights emerging in Egypt and swiftly followed by developments in Lebanon, Syria and Palestine.

Theatre, unlike other forms of literature, depends upon the work of other people besides the author. It also depends upon suitable institutions. When al-Hakim started writing plays, there were few suitably trained actors, directors or theatre staff, and there was no state support for the theatre. This gave rise to the myth that his plays were part of a 'theatre of the mind', being unsuitable, or not meant, for acting, whereas in fact the plays could not be acted because the infrastructure was not in place to stage them. From the 1950s onwards, however, the state both in Egypt and in other Arab countries began to play a role in supporting 'serious' theatre, and by 1966 there were ten state companies working out of nine theatres in Cairo alone. These addressed an audience that had got used to viewing theatre as a form of 'ersatz parliament', in other words as a place for the ventilation of social and political ideas.[28]

M. M. Badawi, from whose *Modern Arabic Drama in Egypt* the above statistics are taken, notes that the new generation of dramatists that emerged to serve this new theatre included some of the most important writers of the time, among them al-Hakim. While the latter's theatrical odyssey took him from realist 'plays on social themes', as a 1950 collection of plays put it, to the introduction of the 'theatre of the Absurd' to Arab audiences through plays such as *The Tree Climber* and *Fate of a Cockroach*,[29] other dramatists such as Nu'man Ashur were experimenting with 'a new note of harsh realism, of urgency and commitment' in plays such as *The People Downstairs* and *The Dughri Family*. Alfred Farag was writing plays influenced by Brecht's epic theatre, such as *Sulayman of Aleppo* and *Ali Jinah of Tabriz*, while Yusuf Idris wrote a landmark play in *al-Farafir*, variously translated as 'The Underlings', or 'Small Fry', which represented an attempt to invent an 'indigenous tradition' for Arab theatre out of pre-modern literary materials like the village *samir*, described by Badawi as 'a popular type of social get-together'. (Farag also drew on materials from *The Arabian Nights* and other pre-modern narratives.) The poet Salah Abd al-Sabur wrote a verse play, *The Tragedy of al-Hallaj*, in 1965 that betrayed the influence of experiments carried out by T. S. Eliot. Arabic drama in the 1960s saw no shortage of experiment.

Aside from the formal qualities of the plays, and the state funds on hand to support them, the drama also had an important social role to play. As noted above, much of the period's prose writing, both before and after the 1967 war, was at least implicitly critical of the regime, a posture of alienation and the making of veiled criticisms being typical of the work of the 'generation of the 1960s'. This was also true of the dramatists, whose work performed a 'cathartic' function: the performance of work that was even indirectly critical of the regime helped to give the impression of public debate, real possibilities for which were curtailed. Thus, al-Hakim's *The Sultan's Dilemma* and *Anxiety Bank*, among other plays, are sometimes read as criticisms of the regime in the same way that Mahfouz's presentation of alienation in his novels from the 1960s, Ibrahim's writing about paralysis, and al-Ghitany's dramatization of blanket fear and censorship have all been seen as the symptoms of a system that, did it but know it, was in a deep state of crisis.[30]

In an environment where everyone was being watched, avant-garde experiment, even the apparent avoidance of political themes in the theatre of the Absurd, could be seen as a political act.

While Egyptian theatre went into decline in the 1970s, many dramatists of the sixties generation either going abroad or ceasing to write, increased resources elsewhere led to the foundation of various public and private-sector theatre companies and to the inauguration of international arts events that served to showcase their work, among them the Baalbek (Lebanon) and Jerash (Jordan) festivals. Cairo itself has hosted an annual Experimental Theatre Festival over the past two decades, serving as a venue for contemporary Arab and international drama.[31] Probably the best-known Arab dramatist of recent decades is the Syrian Saadallah Wannous, an author who, in plays such as *The King is the King,* used traditional stories (in this case from *The Arabian Nights*) to make criticisms of Arab regimes, while at the same time presenting the material in a way that shows his indebtedness both to the dramatists of the Absurd and to Brecht, as mediated by the Egyptian playwrights of the 1960s. Wannous died of cancer in 1997. Before doing so, he published a short 'memoir' of time spent in hospital that mixes present circumstances with memories, fantasies and fragments of unwritten plays.[32]

In this memoir, Wannous writes that 'memories accompany death like voice recordings', and in the drama of his own death he remembers the young man who 'had to speak out against the environment in which I was living ... who looked for the existentialism, the freedom and the beauty that other countries enjoyed. I had to express my irritation at the complications and outworn traditions that obliged us to live poverty-stricken lives. I had to write tracts calling for revolt and liberation and stick them up on people's doors after midnight.' All this once again shows the important 'cathartic' role taken on by modern Arab theatre.

The Contemporary Scene

While it is impossible to be certain about the permanent standing of individual authors, it is perhaps easier to be confident about trends, and three main trends in contemporary Arabic literature will be discussed in this final chapter, various works being considered in relation to them. Most, though by no means all, of the writers mentioned are Egyptian, which suggests that Egypt has managed to retain its leadership of the Arab world in literary matters, for the time being at least. Naturally, many writers of the senior generation continue to be active, including many of those described earlier: Edwar al-Kharrat, Gamal al-Ghitany and Sonallah Ibrahim are all still writing, and to their names can be added those of a host of others, many of them 'sixties writers'. Such names include those of Ibrahim Aslan, Baha Tahir, Mohamed el-Bisatie, Gamal Attia Ibrahim, Ibrahim Abdel-Meguid, Mohamed al-Makhzangi and others. While each of these established authors deserves consideration, this chapter by necessity confines itself to developing trends.

The first of these trends has to do with the connection between contemporary literature and politics. While many Arab writers have been imprisoned by the governments under which they have lived, with others having been either unable to publish or forced to live abroad, today a general weariness of politics seems to have become the norm. This apparent depoliticization is presented either as a variety of postmodern distrust of 'grand narratives' or as a reaction to the climate of religious conservatism that has reigned in the Arab world over recent decades. In this way of looking at things, the turning away from politics is related to disappointment at the failure of earlier aspirations for social and political change or apprehension in the face of current events. Many works, including some of those discussed below, contain evidence of a stifling atmosphere of oppression.

A second trend is the striking growth in the number of women writers, and the increasing interest both in excavating the voices of women from the past and in reflecting on particular features of 'women's writing'. One recent critic, for example, has spoken of what he calls the 'feminization' of the 'literary field' in contemporary Egypt,[1] while others have pointed to the women writers that have emerged in Lebanon, the best known of whom is probably Hanan al-Shaykh.[2] These developments have been accompanied by growing interest in Arab women's writing abroad, which goes some way towards explaining the thinking behind recent translations.

Finally, a third trend, linked to the first two, has been the emphasis placed on individual experience in contemporary writing at the expense of larger, public themes. This 'lyrical' trend, going hand in hand with the deconstruction of large narratives, has led to an emphasis on experience sometimes felt to have been excluded from mainstream literature. There has been a growth in writing dealing more explicitly with sexuality, for example, notably through its treatment of gay themes, as well as a growth in 'regional' or 'ethnic' writing. Writers in Egypt have drawn attention to Nubian identity over recent decades, while the Libyan author Ibrahim al-Koni has

AHMED ALAIDY

BEING
ABBAS
EL ABD

A MODERN ARABIC NOVEL
Translated by Humphrey Davies

written a series of novels drawing attention to the Tuareg people in the Sahara.

Illustrations of postmodernist styles in contemporary Arabic literature can be found in the form and the content of recent texts. One such might be Miral al-Tahawy's *Blue Aubergine*, a novel which could also be discussed in the context of contemporary women's writing.[3] Another might be Ahmed Alaidy's *Being Abbas el Abd*, a stylish debut novel.[4] Al-Tahawy, born in 1968, first attracted attention for *The Tent*, a novel which draws on her Bedouin background,[5] while al-Aidy, an Egyptian author born in Saudi Arabia in 1974, apparently intended *Being Abbas el Abd* to be a kind of anti-novel or comic book and certainly as a text situated outside ordinary literary categories (an influence is Chuck Palahniuk, author of *Fight Club*). Both these novels experiment with reproducing personal experience in the face of confusing social demands, employing a kind of postmodernist collage of different registers of language to do so.

Blue Aubergine, the story of a young woman who bears this nickname, is an assemblage of texts, including memories, fantasies, fragments of dreams, authorial comments, scribbles, interpolated stories and bracketed extracts from a PhD thesis entitled 'The Dialectic of Rebellion and Gender Oppression' that is written in an academic *langue du bois* that is just one of the novel's many styles. These texts, jostling against each other, possess no obvious hierarchy. The narrator's comments, seemingly authoritative, are seen ironically, for example, and the psychological discourse on which they draw is undermined by the surrounding noise. When the narrator intervenes early on in the text to comment that Blue Aubergine will understand her childhood feelings only 'when she has read many pages and drawn lines, as she thumbs through her sources, under the words rebellion and guilt and aggression between the mother and her daughter,' it is suggested that this is just another handy re-description of Blue

Aubergine's confusing experience. It is not authoritative, and it does not trump others. The novel apparently contains no single key.

Nevertheless, individual experience seems to offer a vantage point on the jostling possibilities surrounding Blue Aubergine. 'Our neighbour was the first man to talk to me about Marx and the rotten bourgeoisie and the patriarchal system and sexual freedom. He offered to give me lessons in philosophy and psychology one school year, and then he stuck his hand under the table' and made a pass, she remembers. Personal experience, if not entirely devaluing what the man had to say, at least invites scepticism about it. 'I cried in front of him but he just continued talking about intellectual awareness and self-criticism and the military wing, and imitation and innovation.' Described as 'drowning in the present', Blue Aubergine is assailed by competing political and social discourses, some of them coming from her father's generation and Arab nationalism and socialism ('Abdul Nasser's revolution, that's the only true solution'), some of them filling present horizons with the 'third way' of religious discourse and cultural specificity ('East or West, Islam is best'). Sometimes understanding can be gleaned from reading authoritative-sounding academic texts, reassuring bits of which are spliced into the narrative. The upshot seems to be that though the discourses surrounding Blue Aubergine are more or less devalued and are parts of what is felt to be a threatening linguistic jungle, personal freedom remains a value to aim for, one expressed, for example, in an adolescent dream. 'People came ... looking through the eyes of a woman, bulging and misshapen. She came and did the same thing; she slapped me on the face. "I can look at boys any time I want to," I said. "The streets are full of them."'

Blue Aubergine's demand for self-expression is echoed in al-Aidy's *Being Abbas el Abd*. This novel, told backwards, presents a confused and confusing mass of competing possibilities that include consumer products, drugs, sex, seductive movies, American lifestyles, bits of pan-Arab politics, echoes of nationalism, all of which are zapped through like satellite television channels or product lines in shopping malls. The novel contains a lot of text-messaging on mobile phones, disorientation being the main feature of the street-smart main character's experience. Like *Blue Aubergine*, it is striking both for its assemblage of texts taken from wildly differing discourses, American television to pop psychology, suggesting no significant hierarchy among them, and for the way in which it treats the political, cultural or nationalist thought of previous generations, parodying, misquoting or draining it of meaning by pulling statements out of their original contexts and trivializing them in others. Some of these remain useful as 'great quotes', but on the whole they are revalued (devalued?) in irreverent postmodern terms. Of the political aspirations of previous generations, the narrator comments that Egypt has now 'had its Generation of the Defeat', in other words the generation that fought the Israelis over Palestine. 'We're the generation that came after it. The "I've got nothing left to lose generation". You want us to progress? So burn the history books and forget your precious dead civilization. Stop trying to squeeze the juice from the past.'

Growing interest in 'women's writing' in recent years, particularly from the developing world, has benefited modern Arabic literature, and it has enhanced awareness of this strand of Arab social and intellectual history, both at home in Arab societies themselves and abroad among those interested in Arab cultures and societies. While this is not the place for a survey of Arab feminism, some background may be necessary to understand modern literary writing by Arab women.[6]

The origins of modern Arab feminism are often dated, like so much else, to the period of the *nahda* in Egypt and in particular to the alliance between nationalism and the struggle for women's rights in the work of reformers in the circle around Abdu mentioned in Chapter 2. The work of nationalist and feminist women's organizations, such as the one set up in Cairo in the early decades of the century by the pioneering feminist Huda Sharaawi, was also important in advancing women's causes. Qassem Amin, a member of Abdu's circle, presented the intellectual case for women's rights in the liberal manner adopted by Mill a generation before, and Sharaawi took her cue both from Amin's promotion of women's rights within the context of the struggle for political independence and from contemporary feminist activism in Europe. Her agitation for women's suffrage in Egypt took place at much the same time as that of the suffragettes in Britain; for example, women were demonstrating in the streets of Cairo against the British occupation in 1919, one year after British women over the age of thrity had been given the right to vote.

Amin presented the case for Arab women's rights in two books published at the turn of the century, *The Liberation of Women* and *The New Woman*.[7] In the first of these, he announces that 'I do not believe there is a single educated Egyptian who doubts his country's immense need for reform', adding that this needs to start in the family. 'The status of women,' he says, 'is inseparably tied to the status of a nation', which leads to the proposition that the status of the nation will remain low as long as the status of women within it is low. While 'the Islamic legal system, the *Shari'a*, stipulated the equality of women and men before any other legal system', this original equality has been lost, and men of his generation commonly 'despise' women, destroying their minds by denying them education and trivializing their lives by denying them a role in society's affairs. 'What do you understand a woman to be?' he demands of his (presumably) male readership. 'Like a man, she is a human being.' However, generations of distorted thinking have caused this to be overlooked, with the result that women have become unfit for their roles as wives and mothers. They make poor wives, since a man will 'conceal his joys and sorrows from' an uneducated wife with whom he has little in common. They make imperfect mothers, since they are unable to awaken the intellectual curiosity of their children. At best, such women are 'pleasant pet[s]', Amin says, like the 'angels in the house' that populate the works of Dickens. At worst, a man 'despises [his wife], treats her as nonexistent, and excludes her from his affairs.'

In her discussion of Amin the Egyptian historian Leila Ahmed draws attention to the connections between women's emancipation and national development and between the restoration of the original equality enjoyed by men and women in the Muslim religion and the modernization of the condition of women to bring it into line with international norms. (Amin makes unflattering comparisons between the 'advanced' condition of women in Europe and their 'backwardness' in Arab societies.) These features of his thought place it in the mainstream of the *nahda*: there is the emphasis, for example, on the renovation of Arab society by restoring what has become corrupted and by imitating European models; there is the concern that Arab societies, in imitating Europe, may be in danger of losing part of themselves. These things had the negative effect of suggesting that 'improving the status of women entails abandoning native customs', with resistance to improvement carried out under the impact of western ideas functioning 'as a sign of resistance to imperialism, whether colonial or postcolonial.' Styles of traditional dress, such as the veil, seen by Amin as a sign of female seclusion, were 'tenaciously affirm[ed] as a means of resistance to Western domination,' for example, making women's authenticity dependent on veiling and living in a 'traditional' way.[8]

Concerns of this kind were also raised about the work of Huda Shaarawi, founder and first president of the Egyptian Feminist Union, and president of the Arab Feminist Union on its founding in Cairo in 1944, which had branches throughout the Arab world. Shaarawi and her associates fought for the improvement of women's education and working conditions, as well as for political suffrage. In many of these campaigns she was disappointed, since, as she explains in her memoirs, while women had taken part at the side of men in the struggle for political independence, their 'great acts and endless sacrifices do not change men's views of women'.[9] Sharaawi was born into the aristocracy, and she was, her translator explains, a member of the last generation 'to experience harem life from childhood through mature adulthood'. Women of her class 'lived their lives within the private enclosures of the domestic quarters. When they went out they veiled their faces, thus taking their seclusion with them,' rather in the manner of the Ottoman women described in Pierre Loti's novels. It was while she was on the way back from an international conference in 1923 that Sharaawi publicly removed her veil on her arrival at Cairo railway station. For her, this signalled the casting off of inherited attitudes and the advent of the new woman. For her opponents, it represented a betrayal of authentic ideas of the feminine and the blind imitation of the West. These differing views have resonated down the decades.[10]

Nevertheless, the appearance of female characters in Arabic fiction shows some of the gains that were being made. Mahfouz's novels, for example, are often concerned with the emancipation of women from their traditional roles and the various kinds of stresses to which this could give rise. The expansion of women's roles and life-chances is a major feature of the *Cairo Trilogy*, for example: whereas Amina, wife of Ahmad Abd al-Jawad, lives a highly restricted life in volume one, Sawsan Hammad, fiancée of her grandson Ahmad, is a political activist and feminist in volume three. In works like *Midaq Alley* and *The Beginning and the End* the choices open to women within the family or in the larger social environment are explicitly identified and their narrowness criticized. Both of these novels dramatize the apparent impossibility of escape from the narrow environment of home and family, leading Hamida in the former novel and Nefisa in the latter to despairing, tragic ends.

Even more than Mahfouz, middle-brow writers of the 1950s and 1960s such as the journalist and novelist Ihsan Abdel-Quddus made the throwing off of the constrictions on women's lives into an explicit theme of their writings. One of Abdel-Quddus's best-known novels, for example, *I Am Free*,[11] deals with the struggle of a young woman from a middle-class family to detach herself from inherited *moeurs* and to choose a life to her own liking. It is the freedom to make such choices that allows her to say at the end of this text, 'I am free'. Elsewhere in the Arab world, Leila Baalbaki in Lebanon achieved a *succès d'estime* with her 1957 novel *I Live* and became as representative an author of the period as Françoise Sagan, author of *Bonjour tristesse*, in France. *I Live* dramatized the condition of young women in at least some parts of the Arab world who were finding new paths for themselves in defiance of inherited conceptions of a woman's role and status in society.[12] Baalbaki is also the author of a much-anthologized short story, 'A Spaceship of Tenderness to the Moon';[13] another Lebanese woman writer often compared to Baalbaki and Sagan is Colette Khouri (b. 1937), the author of a novel, *Days with Him*, in which the heroine 'abandons her feckless lover'.[14] Finally, in 1960 the Egyptian novelist Latifa al-Zayyat, less journalistic and more intellectual in profile, published a striking *bildungsroman, The Open Door*, which was taken at the time as summarizing the aspirations of the 'new woman'. She now realized herself in the context of national and political struggle, leaving the private sphere of home and family far behind her.[15]

Yet, despite the interest of this early work it was only in the 1970s in the work of the Egyptian feminist Nawal al-Saadawi and the Moroccan Fatima Mernissi (originally written in French) that Arab feminism began to gain real international exposure. Al-Saadawi is perhaps the best-known contemporary Arab feminist, and many of her books have been translated into English. *Woman at Point Zero*, for example, is a fictional reconstruction of the life of a prostitute,

14. Egyptian feminist and novelist Nawal al-Saadawi

while *The Hidden Face of Eve* is a wide-ranging work on women in the Arab world. Al-Saadawi is also the author of various autobiographical works, among them *Memoirs of a Woman Doctor* and *Memoirs from the Women's Prison*.[16]

These two books present the struggle of Egyptian and Arab women for equal consideration with men through al-Saadawi's memories of her own career. Herself a distinguished physician, at one point holding a senior position in the Egyptian ministry of health, al-Saadawi comments in *Memoirs of a Woman Doctor* on the stilted expectations that hold many women back in the Arab world and on the suffocating framework within which many are condemned to live their lives. Early in her life, she became aware that she was a 'girl'; in other words a potential source of shame. Whereas boys were allowed to do what they liked, girls were shut away indoors, 'as if ... in chains', condemned to the 'hateful, constricted world of women with its permanent reek of garlic and onions'. A conflict developed 'between me and my femininity', and she was 'filled with a great contempt for womankind'. Whereas 'manhood was a distinction and an honour, ... womanhood was a weakness and a disgrace,' the only way out of which being through education. Al-Saadawi chose medicine as a challenge and an escape, as well as a way of proving that she was the equal of any man. Men, in fact, she later discovers, are frauds, their self-confidence merely a reflection of the fact that they, unlike their sisters, mothers or wives, feel that they 'own the past, the present and the future'.[17]

Against masculine posturing al-Saadawi pits 'my strength, my knowledge, [and] my success in my work', qualities that come to the fore in *Memoirs from the Women's Prison*. Arrested in a crackdown against the opposition in September 1981, al-Saadawi was sent to prison. Meeting her fellow prisoners, some of whom are intellectuals but most of whom are not, she draws a connection between the state's authoritarian control of the public sphere and the authority exercised by a father, a brother or a husband over the lives of women in the private sphere of the family. 'Behind every one of these women prisoners is a man: a father branding his daughter for a life of thievery, a husband beating his wife into practising prostitution, a brother threatening his sister so she will smuggle hashish.' Despite their political differences, or, in the case of the non-political prisoners their lack of political awareness, al-Saadawi stages herself as leading a kind of 'feminist revolt' against the policies of the state ('Down with the Open Door Policy, and Camp David, and normalization of relations!

Down with the new colonialism, imperialism, and Zionism!') and the rule of men in general.[18]

It is striking how little reference contemporary Arab women writers make to al-Saadawi. Rather than continuing her activism, their writings seem to be self-absorbed, making only glancing reference to public concerns. Miral al-Tahawy has already been noted in this context, and May Telmissany might also be mentioned, whose novel *Dunyazad* established her as an author to watch.[19] In this short piece, 120 pages all told, Telmissany opens up a 'societal space that male writers have been unable (and perhaps also unwilling) to explore: the complexities of family relationships and especially of gender differences,' in the words of her translator. Organized around the death of a child, Dunyazad, the novel recounts a mother's agonizing grief over her loss. The writing functions both as an attempt to communicate the 'taste, shape, and smell of pain' and as a form of therapy: the story is like a personal diary not meant to be read by others, working instead as a way out of loss. 'Writing Dunyazad,' the author explains, means 'invoking the letters of her name to help me forget.' Dunyazad, the name of Shaharazad's sister in *The Arabian Nights*, has a particular resonance for any woman writer. In the *Nights*, Shaharazad's apparently endless stories save her life, since had her husband not wanted to hear them he could have sent her to the executioner, as he had his previous wives. While Telmissany's narrator is not 'writing for her life' in the way that Shaharazad told stories for hers, the act of writing seems to function as a form of private therapy, a necessary retreat from almost overwhelming concerns. There is an obvious contrast between this kind of writing and that of al-Saadawi, with its advertised commitment to public concerns.

Other Egyptian women authors well known in translation include Alifa Rifaat and Salwa Bakr, both writers of short stories (though Bakr has recently also published a number of novels). The former, unusual because of her positioning outside the ranks of the upper middle classes from which Egypt's women writers mostly come, began to publish late in life following years of writing surreptitiously in defiance of strict family norms. Stories such as 'Thursday Lunch' or 'Me and My Sister' present the loneliness of lower middle-class women either caught in marriages that give them no satisfaction, as in the former, or, like the young woman in the latter, 'sitting at home waiting for someone to come and marry her'. Rifaat's work has attracted comment because of its exploration of sexual themes and the bitter compromises her female characters are sometimes called upon to make, such as in 'Badriyya and Her Husband', in which Badriyya's husband is homosexual ('the wife's the last to know'), or 'An Incident in the Ghobashi Household', which concerns a mother, her daughter and an illegitimate child.[20] Salwa Bakr, younger than Rifaat but from a similar background, has specialized in related subject matter, her stories treating the lives of women for whom, in her translator's words, 'politically, economically and socially life has been set in certain moulds and only with courage can one break out of them,' if one can at all. 'That Beautiful Undiscovered Voice', for example, presents a middle-aged woman who discovers she has a previously undiscovered singing voice. Family circumstances oblige her to deny it. 'The Sorrows of Desdemona' describes the thoughts of a schoolgirl, who, trapped in a narrow family environment, finds temporary outlet for her feelings in school drama lessons, and nowhere else.[21]

Finally, a last set of women writers has emerged in recent decades in Lebanon. One of these, Hoda Barakat, is discussed below; the best known to English-speaking readers is probably Hanan al-Shaykh, though novels by Ghada Samman have also been translated. What links these authors together is their shared experience of the Lebanese civil war, which, starting in 1975 and ending in 1990, left Lebanon devastated and much of its population in exile.[22] It was against this background that women became 'impatient with husbands, brothers, sons and fathers,' in the words of one critic, at least some of whom were caught up in the violence. Women sought to imagine 'a society that no longer posited male ascendancy as the *sine qua non* of future co-existence'. Reflection on the war, its 'catalytic effect', caused such writers to 'recognize ... their previous oppression and marginalization' and to call for the creation of 'a transformed national consciousness' as a result of the unravelling of Lebanese society.[23]

Al-Shaykh's *The Story of Zahra*, for example,[24] describes the life of a young woman originally from the south of Lebanon in war-torn Beirut, where she discovers that the atmosphere of fear has caused people to draw closer to each other, offering new possibilities for affective relations, and that violence has become a way of life, overwhelming human ties. Having fallen in love with a member of one of the city's militias, Zahra's story ends when she is imprisoned and killed by him. Al-Shaykh's later works, including *Women of Sand and Myrrh*, a set of related short stories,[25] and *Only in London*,[26] present women's lives in the Lebanese (and Arab) diaspora, the first set in an unnamed Gulf country, the latter in London. Ghada Samman's *Beirut Nightmares*[27] also records a female narrator's experience of the war, this time in some 150 short sections ('nightmares') that dwell on the chaos and the need to re-evaluate life in the light of it. Trapped in her flat, 'a defenceless noncombatant in the middle of a battlefield', she records the breakdown of normal social relations and the violence that has replaced them, together with the hardening of the barriers between the city's communities. A young man is shot in the street in a revenge attack, 'the only thing that mattered was that he be of a different religion'; her lover, Yousif, is 'killed by armed men at a checkpoint. Just like that, for no reason'; a group of boys are tortured to death, their torturer later sleeping 'as soundly as if he'd conquered five virgins, one after the other'.

These events cause the narrator, modelled on Samman, to question both the pre-war society that had given rise to them, as well as her

15. Beirut during the Lebanese civil war

possible implication in such events. 'You find yourself re-examining everything and the place it's occupied in your life ... [The war] like a masterfully crafted mirror reveals to those who dare to gaze into it the flimsiness of what we call the "bond of human fellowship".' Is she partly responsible for the violence, having previously called for the 'overthrow' of existing society? Is it possible to remain 'neutral' in the face of such events? Whose 'side' is she on?

Recent works of fiction also illustrate marginal forms of sexual identity or minority regional or ethnic identities. There is, for example, the Egyptian writer Alaa Al Aswany's recent *The Yacoubian Building*, mentioned again in the Conclusion to this book, which presents sexual themes with what might be thought to be unusual frankness in today's conservative atmosphere.[28] There is also al-Shaykh's *Women of Sand and Myrrh*, which presents homosexuality among women as a form of sexual manipulation against a background of 'nothing but drinking, eating, telling silly stories, seeing who's got the nicest clothes'. (There is little lesbian presence in modern Arabic literature, and what there is is not valorized; even feminist authors often produce surprisingly conventional representations of sexuality.) While Mahfouz's novels had presented male homosexuality among the working classes (in *Midaq Alley*) and among the upper classes (in *Sugar Street*) as an ordinary part of the Cairene landscape, making contemporary frankness unexceptional except with regard to explorations of female sexuality, more recent works have been written against a different background in which explicitly gay identities have been developed along the lines of what has taken place in the West.

As a result, while neither Al Aswany nor al-Shaykh betrays much sense of the politics of gay identity, as opposed to the presentation of gay characters, identity politics nevertheless form a part of the background to their texts in a way that they do not to those of Mahfouz. This is the case because of the continuing prejudice against men and women who admit homosexual preferences or adopt a gay identity in many Arab societies[29] and because of the development since the 1980s of a politics of gay identity in western societies. It might be added that Mahfouz's presentations of male homosexuality are unapologetic in a way that Al Aswany's are not, and there is no sense in Mahfouz's novels that homosexuality is a foreign contagion, as there is in *The Yacoubian Building*. Indeed, Arab critics have noted the homophobic presentation of gay sexuality in Al Aswany's novel and its conservative 'moral' tone, which is entirely absent from the works of Mahfouz.[30]

Debate on these issues has been set out in a recent book by Brian Whitaker,[31] the terms of which recall debate over women's rights in Arab societies. Is the campaign to bring the treatment of gay and lesbian people into line with international norms guaranteeing non-discrimination and equal rights part of an attempt to force alien standards onto Arab societies, ones which may seem to conflict with the traditions of those societies themselves? One author quoted by Whitaker certainly seems to think so, and he fulminates against the 'Gay International', which is trying to 'impose a European heterosexual regime on Arab men.' Prior to 'the advent of colonialism and Western capital' such men had been content to live their sexual lives spontaneously, unworried by political or identity conceptions about who was 'gay' and who was 'straight'. Hidden behind the 'universal' discourse of human rights that insists on non-discrimination there is an 'orientalist impulse' and an attempt to 'impose' western conceptions of heterosexual or homosexual identity on non-western societies. In reply, Whitaker points out that whatever the theoretical positions involved, what is 'often presented as a choice between cultural authenticity on the one hand', which apparently requires heterosexuality, 'and the adoption of all things Western on the other', which does not, in fact concerns individuals who are often considered either as sinful or as suffering from psychological illness in their own societies. There is also a background of sometimes harsh penal codes.

16. The Yacoubian Building, Cairo, setting for Alaa Al Aswany's novel of the same name, now an international bestseller

The whole question is complicated by the fact that male homosexuality, though stigmatized in contemporary Arab cultures, is represented as a 'natural tendency' and entirely unexceptional in classical Arabic literature, an attitude reflected in the earlier works of Mahfouz. This makes it difficult to see male same-sex desire as culturally inauthentic, or the result of the influence of the West.[32] The real question, Whitaker concludes, is one of individual freedom and of the freedom of both individuals and cultures to develop. This debate seems likely to rumble on and on.

A writer sometimes left out of this discussion is Hoda Barakat. In a series of novels including *The Tiller of Waters* and *The Stone of Laughter*, this Lebanese author resident in Paris has imagined the lives of male homosexuals in Arab societies from within, the first-person narrators of both these works being attracted to men. In *The Tiller of Waters*,[33] for example, the narrator struggles to recreate a familiar space amid the destruction of the Lebanese civil war. Safe in the basement of the destroyed family fabric store, he spreads out the surviving fabrics, rolling in them luxuriantly as he remembers his mother's world, 'composed as it was of a very few windows, all of them firmly closed,' but nevertheless at odds with the masculine hustle of the city outside. In *The Stone of Laughter* the narrator, Kahlil, stares longingly at Naji, a neighbour's son, his 'very black, tangled hair, gleaming beautifully, like his looks'.[34] Conventional styles of Lebanese masculinity, business for the rich, militias for the poor, are closed to Khalil, and, unable to leave his flat because of the snipers on the streets outside, he retreats into obsessive cleaning rituals, trying to construct some sort of haven in the midst of the violence. Barakat has explained that her interest in both novels is in individuals who are 'orphaned' in their own societies, having tried and failed to find a place for themselves outside their communities. Where can such people 'find a place in a world that is split between extremism and moral disintegration,' she asks, as is the case in contemporary Lebanon.[35] From the evidence supplied by these two novels the answer seems to be nowhere.

Contemporary writing has also explored regional identity, two authors in particular, Idris Ali and Haggag Hassan Oddoul, putting Nubian identity onto the literary map in works such as *Dongola* and *Nights of Musk*, respectively.[36] The Nubians, inhabitants of the southernmost areas of Egypt and the northern portions of the Sudan, have their own culture and languages, though most are bilingual in Arabic. They were moved off their lands when these were flooded after the construction of the Aswan High Dam in the 1960s. Other casualties were the Pharoanic temples at Abu Simbel, also moved to prevent inundation. However, as Awad al-Shalali, protagonist of Ali's novel *Dongola*, reflects, while 'the world helped to save the temples' through an international campaign, the Nubian 'people [were left] to their fate'. For men like him this meant menial employment in Egypt's northern cities. Now part of the Nubian diaspora, al-Shalali returns to what is left of Nubia full of bitter memories at the prejudice and exploitation met with in the north. However, once there he discovers that experience in the north has changed him, and that he is accepted only reluctantly by the community.

Oddoul's *Nights of Musk*, a collection of stories, is a more frankly nostalgic, less political work. It too dwells on the loss of Nubia ('Where is our old village? Where is our Nile? Where are our palm trees and our spacious houses?'), with the tone sometimes veering on the folkloric ('long, long ago, south of the rapids, the nights exuded incense and oozed musk'). Nevertheless, Oddoul's stories also ask questions about Nubian identity. Is this simply a matter of looking impotently back on the past and at a community that has all but disappeared, or do Nubians have a future outside their traditional homeland? Both authors write stories of return, and though returning to Nubia can be identity-reinforcing, allowing al-Shalali access to his 'roots' for example, it can also be frustrating because the culture of origin is backward-looking and unable to move forward. These issues dwell somewhere beneath the surface of the first story in Oddoul's collection, for example, in which a boy recounts a visit to his Nubian grandmother. According to her, he is 'gorbatiya', non-Nubian, since though his father is Nubian, his mother is Egyptian, and he is insufficiently black (the Nubians 'are dark, dark, dark, for our sun shines upon our faces'). Yet, who, in reality, is 'a real Nubian', now that '[we've been] pulled up by our roots, and we've become like brushwood'? Part of the answer may depend on extending the limits of Nubian identity, whether in what is left of traditional Nubia or outside it.

Finally, there is Ibrahim al-Koni, a Libyan writer also relevant to the regional theme. In a series of texts of indeterminate genre, long short stories or short novels, al-Koni has presented the experience of the Tuareg people in the southern deserts of Libya and Algeria, spreading into neighbouring Mali and Niger. In *The Bleeding of the Stone*, one of his best-known books,[37] he describes the life of Asouf, a Tuareg herder, who is employed at the rock art sites of Msak Mallat in the southern Sahara guiding parties of 'men and women, old and young, Christians of every sort' on behalf of the state antiquities service. Tuareg society is linked to the desert caravans reaching the area from the south as much as it is to the northern coastlands, and over generations it has developed a relationship of respect mixed with fear with the surrounding desert. Part of this involves the *waddan,* a rare species of mountain sheep that figures as the Tuareg's ancestor and a kind of totemic animal in traditional tales, representing the special covenant that links them with the desert. When two northerners arrive to hunt the *waddan*, Asouf refuses to help them, remembering the covenant that links him with the *waddan* and, through it, with the surrounding desert.

Al-Koni was born in 1948, and he is the author of over forty books, few of which have been translated. He left Libya for Moscow while still a student, and he has lived for many years in Switzerland. His novels interpret Tuareg culture for Arabic-speaking audiences much in the way that works by Ali and Oddoul interpret Nubian culture for them. Together, these three writers have broadened the scope of modern Arabic literature, while drawing attention to the different cultural and linguistic groups living within Arab countries. The Tuareg themselves speak Tamasheq, a kind of Berber, and to outsiders they are probably best known for their practice of male face veiling, Tuareg men wearing elaborate turbans complete with veils that leave only the eyes visible. Al-Koni's novels about them chart the destructive impact of technology on the environment and the destruction of the traditional covenant that binds the human and non-human inhabitants of the desert together.

These 'regional' novels are part of larger trends in contemporary Arabic literature that have seen a turning away from the centre and towards the margins, and from the politically committed literature of the post-war decades towards the experience of individuals, minority groups and women.

Conclusion

At the end of this brief introduction to modern Arabic literature, it may be useful to try to draw together some threads as well as to ask what the immediate prospects for literary writing might be in the Arab world, particularly in the light of developments alluded to earlier in this book and referred to again below.

The literature discussed in this book, and the conception of literature to which it mostly belongs, is a modern development, and the 'pioneers' of modern Arabic literature looked in part to European models, adopting the liberal idea of literature and the writer and producing the 'first novel', the 'first play' and the first examples of modern poetry drawing on modernist experiments that had been underway in Europe. Modern literature thus in some respects meant 'foreign literature', or foreign-influenced literature, and this equation of the modern with the foreign gave rise to debate in the works of Taha Hussein, Yahya Hakki, Tawfiq al-Hakim and others, as we have seen.

More recently, there has been a turning away from European models, and towards elements from the pre-modern literary heritage and from the oral and popular culture. Gamal al-Ghitany has excavated the writings of the Arab historians and pre-modern literary or religious writers, for example, while Tayeb Salih and Naguib Mahfouz in the later part of his career have drawn upon oral traditions and the popular heritage, producing works of 'magical realism'. This part of the story has been one of imitation giving rise to hybridization, as has perhaps been the case in other postcolonial literatures. Another part of it has been the extension of realist or modernist experiments, as in the works of Sonallah Ibrahim and Edwar al-Kharrat.

The contemporary Arab literary scene thus contains the results of various trends, the liberal nationalism of Mahfouz, and the 'commitment' of the post-independence period, giving way first to the growing sense of the autonomy of literature and its critical function in the work of the sixties generation, and then, today, to the various postmodernist, feminist, regional and other trends seeking to express the experiences of the previously marginalized. As is the case elsewhere, postmodernism has found literary expression in narrative fragmentation and an emphasis on self-expression, together with the abandonment of obvious political concerns. In this respect at least, modern Arab literature has found itself aligned with international trends.

However, there has also been another trend pressing on the Arab literary scene over the last two decades or so, and this has been the growing intolerance of literary expression generally, which has made what was always perhaps a minority activity into one that is now that of a sometimes embattled minority. Religious conservatism tends not to value literature on the liberal model – literature, in other words, that carves out a space for intellectual exploration and freedom of expression – since this can challenge religious truths. In the contemporary Arab world writers have been threatened and their works banned as a result of religious pressures, these pressures being possibly stronger than those that in the past used to come from the state. Mahfouz, for example, was attacked in Cairo in 1992 by assailants inspired by a *fatwa*, or religious judgment, against his work by an Islamist preacher. He was badly wounded and lost the use of his right arm. Similarly, Nawal al-Saadawi, one of the Arab world's best-recognized feminist writers, has received threats from religiously inspired elements not sharing her views or not agreeing with her right to express them. Even in the comparatively liberal environment of Cairo, literary works have been withdrawn from sale as a result of religious pressures, pressures that are greater in some other parts of the Arab world. These developments seem to recapitulate campaigns that had once been thought to belong to the history books, such as the campaign mounted by traditionalist elements against Taha Hussein in the 1920s, resulting in the withdrawal of his book on pre-Islamic poetry.[1] While the development of the Internet in recent years has greatly extended possibilities for free expression, both for bloggers and for literary use, there have also been many attempts to police it. When Shohdy Surur, an Egyptian webmaster, published poems by his father Naguib Surur on the Web in 2002, for example, he soon discovered the limits of free expression, being sentenced to one year in prison for offences against 'public morality'.[2]

Long-term observers of the literary scene, such as the critic Pierre Cachia, have written of the special kind of elitism that characterizes modern Arabic literature 'in a part of the world where the majority [was] illiterate and where the modern Renaissance [the *nahda*] was sparked off mainly by contact with European culture.' Moreover, that elitism has sometimes been considered out of touch with what might be called the 'traditional' culture: 'most Arab writers look upon themselves as nothing less than the cultural and social guides of their contemporaries through troubled times,' but the guidance they offer, 'of western origin, ... [is] likely to be shunned by those with a more traditional turn of mind.' While Political Islam has emerged as the most important contemporary social and political trend in the Arab world, able to mobilize populations in a way Arab nationalism no longer seems able to do, 'there is scarcely any sign of approbation or even recognition [of this] in the literature of the elite.' Whereas earlier generations of writers 'patronized the masses but meant well by them', the present generation seems to have lost the confidence that it has anything to say to them, adding to the sense of crisis that reigns in parts of the Arab world.[3] These are Cachia's views. Another more recent survey of the development of modern Arabic literature ends with the comment that 'the outlook for the sort of literature discussed in this volume remains a somewhat precarious one'.[4]

Nevertheless, literature continues to get written, and readers continue to read it, and recent decades have even seen an increase in the outlets and the money available to authors, following the expansion of the media and literary publication in the Gulf. Moreover, many more Arab writers have successfully made a name for themselves outside their countries of origin and in translation, and some of them have even managed to escape the traditional niches into which Arab authors have tended to be put, as was noted in Chapter 1. In concluding this book, one could do worse than consider the fortunes of two recent novels, popular in the Arab world, which have also struck chords with western readers and which seem to augur well for the continuing vitality of Arabic literature. These novels, *Gate of the Sun* by the Lebanese writer and journalist Elias Khoury, and *The Yacoubian Building* by the Egyptian writer Alaa Al Aswany, already mentioned in Chapter 6, conform to conceptions of literature outlined in this book, while also suggesting that Arabic literature has now become a literature like any other as far as international readers are concerned. Humphrey Davies's translation of *Gate of the Sun* won the UK Banipal Prize for Arabic Translation in 2006, for example, while *The Yacoubian Building* has become an international bestseller, a first for any novel originally written in Arabic.[5]

Khoury, born in Lebanon, has dealt in his work with the fortunes of that country and with the experience of Palestinians made homeless by the declaration of the state of Israel in 1948, the year in which he was born. *Gate of the Sun* gives a panorama of this experience, including references to events in 1936, 1948, 1970 and 1971 and after 1975 during the civil war in Lebanon. It does this through the character of Khaleel, a doctor in a refugee camp in Beirut charged with taking care of Yunis, a Palestinian fighter on his deathbed. Yunis's career seems to recapitulate Khaleel's own experiences and those of his generation, but how do these fading memories of a dying man relate to the present? Can a coherent story be made out of them that can serve as a guide for the future? The novel, Khoury notes, is a relatively new literary genre in Lebanon, as it is elsewhere in the Arab world, but it is one in which history can be written on a human scale and historical themes given concrete expression. While 'Lebanon's new ruling class wants to make the country part of the petro-dollar system and to convert it into a small Hong Kong,' he says, there are other options including making the country 'part of the search for democracy, identity and change in the Arab world.'⁶ His novel, designed to be part of the exploration of those other options, shows Khoury taking seriously his role as the conscience of the nation.

Al Aswany's *The Yacoubian Building* also deals with history, though this time the focus is Egypt. He introduces easily recognizable characters and presents social issues in concrete form, and as a result it has much in common with popular forms of television drama, as critics have noted. It cannot have done the book any harm either that the Yacoubian Building of the title in fact exists (it is an apartment building located in a mixed commercial district), and it is easy to imagine Al Aswany's characters crossing each other on this building's stairway as they do in the pages of the novel. Among these characters are Zaki Bey el-Dessouki, an impoverished representative of the class that ruled Egypt until the country's 1952 Revolution, various members of the *nouveaux riches* who have profited from the country's opening to the international capitalist system from the 1970s onwards, and representatives of the country's increasingly pauperized lower-middle and working classes. There is also Taha el Shazli, whose story draws attention to the restricted options available to young people: the son of the building's doorman, his ambitions to become a police officer founder because of his modest social origins and he is drawn towards extremist violence. Al Aswany's novel draws attention to the atmosphere of nostalgia that seems to have taken hold in today's Egypt, idealizing the past in contrast to a disappointing present and to a future that seems blocked. Above all, he illustrates the makeshift compromises that almost all the characters have to resort to in order to get by in a society in which corruption has become rife, notably in politics and the business world, making life, for many, into a kind of bitter choice between poverty or emigration. A second novel by Al Aswany, *Chicago*, was published in Cairo in 2007, and it cannot be long before this too is available in translation.[7]

These novels, the one filling a large canvas and dealing with post-war Palestinian experience, the other describing life in a Cairo apartment building, are as good an introduction as any to contemporary Arabic literature. Both books focus on issues such as the meanings to be found in the past, the options available for the present, and the often cruel predicaments in which men and women from various social backgrounds find themselves. Khoury's novel, postmodernist in its use of narrative and its 'polyphonic' texture, compares interestingly with the more straightforward realism employed by Al Aswany. Yet, the issues these novels raise, and the literary conceptions on which they draw, are perhaps the bread and butter of modern Arabic literature.

Notes

Introduction

1. In his *Modern Arabic Literature in Translation: A Companion* (London: Saqi, 2005), Salih Altoma even speaks of a 'linguistic iron curtain' separating the Arab world from the West.
2. Suggestions for further reading are also given at the end of this book.
3. Soueif is the author of *The Map of Love*, shortlisted for the Booker Prize in 1999. Matar's *The Season of Men*, a Libyan memoir, was shortlisted for the same prize in 2006. Ghali's novel was published in 1964 (London: Andre Deutsch). An Arabic translation was published in Cairo in 2007.
4. Franck Mermier's *Le Livre et la ville, Beyrouth et l'édition arabe* (Arles: Actes sud, 2005) is a useful recent account of Arab publishing.
5. Salih Altoma (*Modern Arabic Literature in Translation*, London: Saqi, 2005) gives statistics for English translations of Arabic fiction between 1947 and 2003: 'most of the 322 titles listed ... (about 170 titles) are Egyptian. The remaining titles represent: Algeria (2), Iraq (11), Jordan (3), Kuwait (1), Lebanon (26), Libya (7), Morocco (8), Palestine (22), Saudi Arabia (11), Sudan (5), Syria (11), Tunisia (2), United Arab Emirates and Yemen (2).'
6. *Modern Arabic Literature*, edited by M. M. Badawi (Cambridge: Cambridge University Press, 1992).
7. *L'Écrivain* (Paris: Julliard, 2001). The names are Franco-Algerian transliterations of those of Egyptian writers and intellectuals. Khadra is the author of detective novels featuring Commissioner Brahim Llob of the

Algiers Police Department. Originally written in French, some of them have been translated into English.

8. *Comme un été qui ne reviendra pas, Le Caire 1955–1996* (Arles: Actes sud, 2001). Berrada gives the names of Egyptian musicals from the 1940s, which starred singers such as those he mentions. Taha Hussein, Tawfiq el-Hakim, [al-] Manfalouti and Ahmed Lutfi el-Sayyed are Egyptian writers.

9. Robert Irwin, in a review of Salma Khadra Jayyusi, ed., *Modern Arabic Fiction: An Anthology* (New York: Columbia University Press, 2005), that appeared in the *London Review of Books* (18 August 2005).

10. Mermier (*Le Livre et la ville,* 2005) describes publishing across the Arab world, focusing on centres like Cairo and Beirut. Readership figures for Egyptian authors are suggested in R. Jacquemond, *Entre scribes et écrivains: le champ littéraire dans l'Egypte contemporaine* (Arles: Actes sud, 2003), an indispensable guide. An English translation of this book is due from the American University in Cairo Press in 2008.

Reading Arabic Literature

1. Quotations from E. Said, *Orientalism* (London: Penguin, 1995).

2. See Robert Irwin's *For Lust of Knowing: the Orientalists and their Enemies* (London: Allen Lane, 2006).

3. Denys Johnson-Davies, 'On Translating Arabic Literature' in Ferial J. Ghazoul and Barbara Harlow (eds.), *The View from Within: Writers and Critics on Contemporary Arabic Literature* (Cairo: AUC Press, 1994). The same author's *Memories in Translation: A Life Between the Lines of Arabic Literature* (Cairo: AUC Press, 2006) contains additional discussion.

4. Suzanne Jill Levine, 'The Latin American novel in English translation' in Efrain Kristal (ed.), *The Cambridge Companion to the Latin American Novel* (Cambridge: Cambridge University Press, 2005).

5. Salih J. Altoma, *Modern Arabic Literature in Translation* (London: Saqi, 2005).

6. Robin Waterfield in *Prophet: the Life and Times of Kahalil Gibran* (London: Allen Lane, 1998).

7. 'In the States, as of April 1996, [Gibran's] *The Prophet* had sold over 9,000,000 copies since publication ... In the rest of the English-speaking world, about another 25,000 copies are sold every year.' These figures make Gibran not only the most successful Arab writer ever, but also 'probably the best-selling individual poet of all time after Shakespeare and Lao-tzu' (Waterfield).

8. R. Jacquemond, *Entre scribes et écrivains: le champ littéraire dans l'Egypte contemporaine* (Arles: Actes sud, 2003), chapter 5.

9. Jacquemond, *Entre scribes et écrivains*, 2003, p. 157. Jacquemond extends his

discussion in 'Translation and Cultural Hegemony: the Case of French–Arabic Translation' in L. Venuti (ed.), *Rethinking Translation: Discourse, Subjectivity, Ideology* (London: Routledge, 1992), pp. 139–158.

10. Robert Irwin in *The Arabian Nights: A Companion* (London: Tauris, 2003).

11. André Lefevere discusses nineteenth-century Arabic translation in *Translation, Rewriting and the Manipulation of Literary Fame* (London: Routledge, 1992), chapter 6, 'The Case of the Missing Qasidah'.

12. A. J. Arberry (ed. and trans.), *Modern Arabic Poetry: An Anthology with English Verse Translations* (Cambridge: Cambridge University Press, 1967).

13. Naguib Mahfouz, *Palace Walk*, trans. William Maynard Hutchins et al. (New York & London: Alfred A. Knopf, 2001).

14. Tayeb Salih, *Season of Migration to the North*, trans. Denys Johnson-Davies (London: Penguin, 2003).

15. Al-Khidr, or al-Khadir, meaning 'the green man', appears in the *Qur'an* (sura 18) as a guide, subsequently appearing in popular stories and legends. The meaning of al-Khidr's enigmatic behaviour has been the subject of generations of commentary. See the article by A. J. Wensinck, 'al-Khadir (al-Khidr)' in *The Encyclopaedia of Islam*, edited by P. Bearman, Th. Bianquis, C.E. Bosworth, E. van Donzel and W.P. Heinrichs (Leiden: Brill, 2007 [Brill Online]).

16. Appearances of Solomon in the *Qur'an* are detailed in J. Walker, 'Sulayman b. Dawud ' in *The Encyclopaedia of Islam* (Leiden: Brill, 2007 [Brill Online]).

17. *The Arabian Nights*, vol. 2, trans. Husain Haddawy (New York: Alfred A. Knopf [Everyman's Library], 1998).

18. Gamal al-Ghitany, *Le Livre des illuminations* (Paris: Seuil, 2005), trans. Khaled Osman, who supplies a lengthy introduction and notes.

19. See Jaroslav Stetkevych, *The Modern Arabic Literary Language: Lexical and Stylistic Developments* (Chicago: University of Chicago Press, 1970).

20. The prefaces and postscripts al-Hakim wrote to his plays set out the linguistic issues. See W. M. Hutchins (ed. and trans.), *The Plays, Prefaces and Postscripts of Tawfiq al-Hakim: Vol. 2, Theater of Society* (Washington: Three Continents Press, 1984), esp. pp. 337–342.

21. Tahir Wattar, *The Earthquake*, trans. Bill Granara (London: Saqi, 2000); Mohamed Choukri, *For Bread Alone*, trans. Paul Bowles (London: Telegram, 2006). The Moroccan novelist Tahar Ben Jelloun's French translation of the latter work is published as *Le Pain nu* (Paris: Seuil, 1998). For Laredj, see *Fleurs d'Amandier* trans. Catherine Charrauau (Arles: Actes sud, 2001), and *Le Livre de l'Émir*, trans. Marcel Bois (Arles: Actes sud, 2006).

22. See Mermier's study (*Le Livre et la ville*, 2005), from which this information is taken. Jacquemond's (*Entre scribes et écrivains*, 2003) is one of the few books available on the sociology of literature in the Arab world.

23. See Jacquemond (*Entre scribes et écrivains*, 2003), Mermier (*Le Livre et la ville*, 2005) and Marina Stagh, *The Limits of Freedom of Speech: Prose Literature and Prose Writers in Egypt under Nasser and Sadat* (Stockholm: Almqvist & Wiksell, 1993), for discussion.

24. Elleke Boehmer's *Colonial and Postcolonial Literature* (Oxford: Oxford University Press, 1995) is a useful introduction.

25. Translation studies are introduced by Susan Bassnett-McGuire in *Translation Studies* (London: Routledge, 2002).

26. F. Moretti, 'Conjectures on World Literature', *New Left Review*, January–February 2000, pp. 54–68; further articles appearing in 2003 and 2004. See also the same author's edited collection, *The Novel* (2 vols., Princeton: Princeton University Press, 2006), originally published in Italian.

27. Pascale Casanova, *La République mondiale des lettres* (Paris: Seuil, 1999).

The Modern Element

1. Quotations from Robert Solé, *Bonaparte à la conquete de l'Egypte* (Paris: Seuil, 2006). The 'Mamluks' were members of a distinct caste that then ruled Egypt under nominal Ottoman suzerainty.

2. See Albert Hourani, *A History of the Arab Peoples* (London: Faber & Faber, 2002), chapters 16–20.

3. Bernard Lewis describes attempts to modernize Ottoman society, including the Empire's Arab provinces, in *The Emergence of Modern Turkey* (Oxford: Oxford University Press, 1961), chapters 3–5. Albert Hourani surveys the intellectual background to modernization in *Arabic Thought in the Liberal Age* (Oxford: Oxford University Press, 1962).

4. Ibrahim Abu-Lughod, *The Arab Rediscovery of Europe* (Princeton: Princeton University Press, 1963).

5. Quotations from Pierre Cachia, *Taha Husayn: His Place in the Egyptian Literary Renaissance* (London: Luzac, 1956).

6. The three volumes are available in an omnibus edition published by the American University in Cairo Press (1997). They include *An Egyptian Childhood* (trans. E. H. Paxton), *The Stream of Days* (trans. Hilary Wayment) and *A Passage to France* (trans. Kenneth Cragg).

7. Hourani (*Arabic Thought in the Liberal Age*, 1962) gives context and background on Taha Hussein.

8. Sabry Hafez's *Genesis of Arabic Narrative Discourse* (London: Saqi, 1993) notes 'the interaction between the awakening of national consciousness, the

composition of the reading public, its role in the creation of the new sensibility and the rise of narrative genres' in the period.

9. The *locus classicus* for the growth of Arab nationalism in the early decades of the twentieth century is Georges Antonius, *The Arab Awakening*, first published in the 1930s. Hourani gives a more up-to-date view (Hourani, *A History of the Arab Peoples*, 2002).

10. Yehia Hakki, *The Lamp of Umm Hashim*, trans. Denys Johnson-Davies (Cairo: AUC Press, 2004). There is an earlier translation by M. M. Badawi (Leiden: Brill, 1973).

11. Granddaughter of the Prophet Mohamed and sister of al-Hussein, Sayeda Zeinab sought refuge in Cairo following the latter's defeat at the battle of Karbala in 680 CE (see footnote 4 to the next chapter). She is buried at the site where her mosque now stands.

12. Hakki's relationship to the Arab *nahda* is explored in Miriam Cooke's study, *The Anatomy of an Egyptian Intellectual* (Washington: Three Continents Press, 1984).

13. Tawfiq al-Hakim, *The Prison of Life*, trans. Pierre Cachia (Cairo: AUC Press, 1992).

14. Tawfiq al-Hakim, *Return of the Spirit* and *Diary of a Country Prosecutor*, trans. William Hutchins (Washington: Three Continents Press, 1990) and Abba Eban (London: Saqi, 2005), respectively. Eban's translation first appeared under the title *Maze of Justice* in 1947.

15. Paul Starkey's *From the Ivory Tower* is particularly good on al-Hakim's conception of literature and his relation to the Egyptian and Arab environment (London: Ithaca Press, 1987).

16. S. Somekh in 'The Neo-classical Arabic Poets' in M. M. Badawi (ed.), *Modern Arabic Literature* (Cambridge: Cambridge University Press, 1992), pp. 36–81. The quotations are from this essay.

17. R. C. Ostle, 'The Romantic Poets', in M. M. Badawi (ed.), *Modern Arabic Literature* (Cambridge: Cambridge University Press, 1992), pp. 82–131. Further quotations from this essay appear later in this paragraph.

The Novel and the New Poetry

1. Naguib Mahfouz, *Midaq Alley* and *The Beginning and the End*, trans. Trevor Le Gassick (London: Heinemann, 1976) and Ramses Awad, respectively (Cairo: American University in Cairo Press, 1984).

2. These novels, translated by William Maynard Hutchins et al., are available in an omnibus edition (New York: Knopf, 2001).

3. Sassoon Somekh provides details of Mahfouz's career in his *The Changing Rhythm* (Leiden: Brill, 1973), which deals with all the novels published until the end of the 1960s.

4. The mosque of al-Husayn, or al-Hussein, is opposite al-Azhar in Cairo. Hussein, grandson of the Prophet Mohamed, was killed at Karbala in what is now Iraq in 680 CE. His body is sometimes said to be buried in Karbala, his head in Cairo. (See L. Veccia Vaglieri, '(al-) Husayn b. 'Ali b. Abi Talib' in the *Encyclopaedia of Islam*, edited by P. Bearman, Th. Bianquis, C. E. Bosworth, E. van Donzel and W. P. Heinrichs (Leiden: Brill, 2007 [Brill Online]).

5. Naguib Mahfouz, *Children of the Alley*, trans. Peter Theroux (New York: Doubleday, 1996). There is an older translation by Philip Stewart, published as *Children of Gebelaawi* (London: Heinemann, 1981).

6. See Marina Stagh, *The Limits of Freedom of Speech*, 1993, an indispensable guide. Somekh's 'The Sad Millenarian: An Examination of Awlad Haratina' is a critical evaluation, collected in Trevor Le Gassick (ed.), *Critical Perspectives on Naguib Mahfouz* (Washington: Three Continents Press, 1991), pp. 101–114.

7. English translations of all Mahfouz's novels appeared following his award of the Nobel Prize for Literature in 1988.

8. Naguib Mahfouz, *Miramar*, trans. Fatma Moussa-Mahmoud (London: Heinemann, 1978).

9. Fathy Ghanem, *The Man Who Lost His Shadow*, trans. Desmond Stewart (Cairo: AUC Press, 1994 [1966]).

10. *Respected Sir* and *Wedding Song* are available in the Doubleday/AUC Press series (trans. Rasheed el-Enany and Olive E. Kenny, respectively). *Karnak Café* has been translated by Roger Allen (Cairo: AUC Press, 2007).

11. Naguib Mahfouz, *Mirrors*, trans. Roger Allen (Cairo: AUC Press, 2000).

12. Rasheed el-Enany calls these 'episodic novels' in a recent study (*Naguib Mahfouz: The Pursuit of Meaning*, London: Routledge, 1993), describing their experimentation with traditional Arab literary forms. All three novels are available from Doubleday and AUC: *The Harafish* translated by Catherine Cobham (1994), and *Arabian Nights and Days* and *The Journey of Ibn Fattouma* translated by Denys Johnson-Davies (1995 and 1992).

13. Kadhim Jihad Hassan, *Le Roman arabe* (Arles: Actes sud, 2006).

14. See the autobiographical piece, written in English in 1983, in Roger Allen (ed.), *Critical Perspectives on Yusuf Idris* (Washington: Three Continents Press, 1994).

15. The English translation of *The Cheapest Nights* (Cairo: AUC Press, 1990) by Wadida Wassef includes stories taken from five short-story collections published in Cairo in the 1950s and 1960s. 'The Stranger' and 'The Black Policeman' are in *Rings of Burnished Brass*, trans. Catherine Cobham (Cairo: AUC Press, 1990).

16. The quotations in these paragraphs are taken from P. M. Kurpershoek's study *The Short Stories of Yusuf Idris: A Modern Egyptian Author*

(Leiden: Brill 1981). The Cairo Arabic Language Academy was founded in 1934, taking the Academie Française as a model and carrying out similar functions. Rather like the French Academy, the Cairo body can appear to be detached from actual usage. There are similar bodies in Damascus and elsewhere.

17. The quotation is from Taha Hussein and is taken from M. M. Badawi, 'Commitment in Contemporary Arabic Literature' in Issa J. Boullata (ed.), *Critical Perspectives on Modern Arabic Literature* (Washington: Three Continents Press, 1980), pp. 23–44.

18. Abdel Rahman al-Sharqawi, *Egyptian Earth*, trans. Desmond Stewart (London: Saqi, 1990 [1962]).

19. Salih's work has been translated into English by Denys Johnson-Davies, including *The Wedding of Zein and Other Stories* (London: Heinemann, 1969), *Season of Migration to the North* (London: Penguin, 2003) and *Bandarshah* (London: Kegan Paul/UNESCO, 1996).

20. See Jabra Ibrahim Jabra, 'Modern Arabic Literature and the West' in Issa J. Boullata (ed.), *Critical Perspectives on Modern Arabic Literature* (Washington: Three Continents Press, 1980), pp. 7–22.

21. Quotations from Wail S. Hassan, *Tayeb Salih. Ideology and the Craft of Fiction* (Syracuse, NY: Syracuse University Press, 2003).

22. Abdelrahman Munif, *Cities of Salt*, trans. Peter Theroux (New York: Vintage, 1989); *The Trench*, trans. Peter Theroux (New York: Vintage, 1993) and *Variations on Night and Day*, trans. Peter Theroux (New York: Vintage, 1993).

23. Sabry Hafez, 'An Arabian Master', *New Left Review* 37, January–February 2006, pp. 39–68. There is a French translation of *East of the Mediterranean* (Paris: Sindbad, 1985).

24. 'Abd al-Rahman Munif, *Endings*, trans. Roger Allen (New York: Interlink, 2005).

25. Neither of these works, published in Arabic in 1999 (*Land of Darkness*) and 2004 (*Notes on History and Resistance*), has been translated into English. The quotation is from Sabry Hafez ('An Arabian Master', *New Left Review* 37, January–February 2006, pp. 39–68). See also Abdel-Khaleq Farouq's review of the latter book in *al-Ahram Weekly* (Cairo), 18 March 2004, at http://weekly.ahram.org.eg/2004/682/b01.htm

26. Abd al-Rahman Munif, *Story of a City: A Childhood in Amman*, trans. Samira Kawar (London: Quartet, 1996).

27. This account is indebted to Salma Khadra Jayyusi's *Trends and Movements in Modern Arabic Poetry* (Leiden: Brill, 1977). The first volume of this two-volume work contains an account of Arabic poetry more or less up to the outbreak of the Second World War. The second volume, from which the

quotations in this and following paragraphs are taken, takes the story up to the 1970s.

28. See Abdul Wahab al-Bayati, *Love, Death and Exile*, trans. Bassam K. Frangieh (Washington: Georgetown University Press, 1990), a bilingual selection of poems.

29. Adonis, *Introduction to Arab Poetics*, trans. Catherine Cobham (London: Saqi, 1990).

30. A convenient anthology of post-war Arabic poetry is *Modern Poetry of the Arab World* (London: Penguin, 1985), edited and translated by Abdullah al-Udhari, which contains versions of the poems mentioned. *Modern Arab Poets*, edited and translated by Issa J. Boullata (London: Heinemann, 1976) is similar, focusing on poetry published between 1950 and 1975. Salma Khadra Jayyusi's *Anthology of Modern Arabic Poetry* (New York: Columbia University Press, 1987) is a larger work and contains an introduction summarizing views presented in her *Trends and Movements in Modern Arabic Poetry* (Leiden: Brill, 1977).

31. Jayyusi in her *Trends and Movements in Modern Arabic Poetry* (Leiden: Brill, 1977).

Occupation and Diaspora: the Literature of Modern Palestine

1. See Ilan Pappe, *A History of Modern Palestine* (Cambridge: Cambridge University Press, 2004), esp. chapters 4 and 5.

2. Ghassan Kanafani, *Men in the Sun*, trans. Hilary Kirkpatrick (London: Heinemann, 1978) and *All That's Left to You*, trans. May Jayyusi and Jeremy Reed (Cairo: AUC Press, 1992).

3. Emile Habiby, *Secret Life of Saeed the Pessoptimist*, trans. Salma Khadra Jayyusi and Trevor Le Gassick (London: Zed, 1985).

4. Pappe (*A History of Modern Palestine*, 2004, chapter 5) gives details of the discrimination Palestinian refugees faced, and face, in many Arab countries.

5. Halim Barakat, *Six Days*, trans. Bassam Frangieh and Scott McGehee (Washington: Three Continents Press, 1990).

6. Halim Barakat, *Days of Dust*, trans. Trevor Le Gassick (Washington: Three Continents Press, 1983).

7. Fadwa Tuqan, *A Mountainous Journey*, trans. Olive Kenny (London: Women's Press, 1990).

8. A second volume has appeared in French: *Le Cri de la Pierre*, trans. Joséphine Lama and Benoît Tadié (Paris: L'asiathèque, 1998).

9. Jabra Ibrahim Jabra, *The First Well*, trans. Issa J. Boullata (Fayetteville: University of Arkansas Press, 1995).

10. Jabra Ibrahim Jabra, *The Search for Walid Masoud*, trans. Roger Allen and Adnan Haydar (Syracuse: Syracuse University Press, 2000).

11. Jabra Ibrahim Jabra, *Princesses' Street*, trans. Issa J. Boullata (Fayetteville: University of Arkansas Press, 2005).

12. Legal, political and social issues surrounding the Palestinian refugees are examined in Farouk Mardam-Bey and Elias Sanbar (eds.), *Le Droit au Retour: le problème des réfugiés palestiniens* (Arles: Actes sud, 2002).

13. Sahar Khalifeh, *Wild Thorns*, trans. Trevor Le Gassick and Elizabeth Fernea (Northampton, Mass.: Interlink, 2003).

14. See Pappe, *A History of Modern Palestine*, 2004, chapters 6 and 7.

15. Winner of the Naguib Mahfouz Medal for Literature (American University in Cairo). The English translation (Cairo: AUC Press, 2000) is by Ahdaf Soueif.

16. See the anthologies by al-Udhari and Jayyusi (1986 and 1987), mentioned earlier. There is a book of selected poems translated by Munir Akash et al. (*Unfortunately it was Paradise*, Berkeley: University of California Press, 2003) and an earlier one translated by Denys Johnson-Davies (*The Music of Human Flesh*, London: Heinemann, 1980). The best place to start is al-Udhari's *Victims of a Map* (London: Saqi, 2005), a bilingual anthology of poetry by Darwish, Adonis and Samih al-Qasim.

17. Mahmoud Darwish, *Memory for Forgetfulness*, trans. Ibrahim Muhawi (Berkeley: University of California Press, 1995).

18. Mahmoud Darwish, *Le Palestine comme métaphore* (Arles: Actes sud, 1997).

Disillusion and Experiment

1. The story is in *The Time and the Place and Other Stories*, trans. Denys Johnson-Davies (New York: Doubleday, 1992), containing stories published in Cairo from the 1950s to 1980s.

2. Stefan G. Meyer, *The Experimental Arab Novel* (Buffalo: State University of New York, 2001).

3. Samia Mehrez, *Egyptian Writers between History and Fiction: Essays on Naguib Mahfouz, Sonallah Ibrahim, and Gamal al-Ghitani* (Cairo: AUC Press, 1994).

4. Sonallah Ibrahim, *The Smell of It*, trans. Denys Johnson-Davies (London: Heinemann, 1971).

5. See Mehrez, *Egyptian Writers between History and Fiction* (1994) for publication history and the quotation from Ibrahim. Stagh (*The Limits of Freedom of Speech*, 1993) describes the controversy in detail.

6. Sonallah Ibrahim, *The Committee*, trans. May St Germain and Charlene Constable (Syracuse, NY: Syracuse University Press, 2001) and *Zaat*, trans. Anthony Calderbank (Cairo: AUC Press, 2001).

7. Ibrahim may be making a joke here: many Arab public figures have awarded themselves doctorates.

8. See Bertolt Brecht, *Brecht on Theatre*, trans. John Willett (London: Methuen, 1978).

9. Included in the English translation of *The Smell of It*.

10. Sonallah Ibrahim, *Dhat* (Cairo: Dar al-mustaqbal al-arabi, 1992).

11. Sonallah Ibrahim, *Bayrut, Bayrut* (Cairo: Dar al-mustaqbal al-arabi, 1988).

12. French translations are available: Sonallah Ibrahim, *Charaf, ou l'honneur* (Arles: Actes sud, 1999) and *Amrikanli: un automne à San Francisco* (Arles: Actes sud, 2005).

13. Thus Frédéric Lagrange: modern Arabic 'literature often displaces the shock of the encounter with the West into the arena of sexuality … homosexual sexuality [appearing] as a sign of decay … in the literature of leftist and nationalist writers' and contributing to the 'normalization' of sexuality in present Arab societies. ('Male Homosexuality in Modern Arabic Literature', in Mai Ghoussoub and Emma Sinclair-Webb (eds.), *Imagined Masculinities: Male Identity and Culture in the Modern Middle East*, London: Saqi, 2000, pp. 169–198).

14. Sonallah Ibrahim, *al-Talasus* (Cairo: Dar al-mustaqbal al-arabi, 2007).

15. Gamal al-Ghitany, *Zayni Barakat*, trans. Farouk Abdel-Wahab (London: Penguin, 1988). The other work is *Pyramid Texts*, trans. Anthony Calderbank (Cairo: AUC Press, 2007).

16. Gamal al-Ghitany, *What Happened in al-Maqshara*, trans. Mona Anis and David Tresilian, in *Cairo Today*, April 1992.

17. Egypt was conquered by the Ottomans in 1517.

18. Mehrez (*Egyptian Writers between History and Fiction*, 1994) calls the pastiche of historical styles in *Zayni Barakat* 'a symbolic act against the censor … [since] there is no "I" to be held responsible' for the novel's political content.

19. Edwar al-Kharrat, *City of Saffron* and *Girls of Alexandria* are translated by Frances Liardet (London: Quartet, 1989 and 1993, respectively). *Rama and the Dragon* is translated by Ferial J. Ghazoul and John Verlenden (Cairo: AUC Press, 2003).

20. Quotations from al-Kharrat's essay 'The Mashriq' in R. Ostle (ed.), *Modern Literature in the Near and Middle East, 1850–1970* (London: Routledge, 1991), pp. 180–192.

21. See the pieces by Adorno, Benjamin, Bloch, Brecht, Lukacs and others in Ernst Bloch et al., *Aesthetics and Politics* (London: Verso, 2007).

22. Quotations from Jayyusi's 'Modernist Poetry in Arabic' in M. M. Badawi (ed.), *Modern Arabic Literature* (op. cit., 1992), pp. 132–179. In her anthology *Modern Arabic Poetry* (New York: Columbia University

Press, 1987), Jayyusi writes of the 'crisis' and 'metaphorical chaos' of Arabic poetry in the 1970s.

23. Ferial Ghazoul and John Verlenden. The quotation is from the introduction to Matar's *Quartet of Joy* (Fayetteville: University of Arkansas Press, 1997).

24. On Nigm and the 'ibn al-balad', see Kamal Abdel-Malek, *A Study of the Vernacular Poetry of Ahmad Fu'ad Nigm* (Leiden: Brill, 1990). Nigm has since moved from al-Darb al-Ahmar to Mouqatem in the hills outside Cairo, where he now has a mobile phone.

25. Marilyn Booth's article 'Poetry in the Vernacular' in M. M. Badawi (ed.), *Modern Arabic Literature* (Cambridge: Cambridge University Press, 1992), pp. 463–482, surveys the field.

26. Quotations from M. M. Enani (trans.), *Angry Voices: An Anthology of the Off-Beat Egyptian Poets* (Fayetteville: University of Arkansas Press, 2003).

27. European dramatists have looked to classical models for inspiration, but there is nothing comparable in the history of Arabic literature. The quotation, like those that follow, is from M. M. Badawi, *Modern Arabic Drama in Egypt* (Cambridge: Cambridge University Press, 1987).

28. The theatre of the period is vividly described by an American visitor to Cairo at the time. See Irving Brown, 'The Effervescent Egyptian Theatre' in Boullata (ed.), *Critical Perspectives on Modern Arabic Literature*, 1980, pp. 332–340.

29. Tawfiq al-Hakim, *The Tree Climber* and *Fate of a Cockroach*, both trans. Denys Johnson-Davies (London: Oxford University Press, 1966 and London: Heinemann, 1973, respectively).

30. Sabry Hafez describes the atmosphere of the decade in his 'The Egyptian Novel in the Sixties' in Boullata (ed.), *Critical Perspectives on Modern Arabic Literature*, 1980, pp. 171–187.

31. The Egyptian critic Nehad Selaiha writes a column in English in the Cairo newspaper *al-Ahram Weekly* that is essential reading for anyone interested in Egyptian and Arab theatre (www.ahram.org.eg/weekly)

32. Saadallah Wannous, *Une mort éphémère*, trans. Rania Samara (Arles: Actes sud, 2001).

The Contemporary Scene

1. Jacquemond in *Entre scribes et écrivains* (2003).

2. See Miriam Cooke, *War's Other Voices: Women Writers on the Lebanese Civil War* (Syracuse: Syracuse University Press, 1996).

3. Miral al-Tahawy, *Blue Aubergine*, trans. Anthony Calderbank (Cairo: AUC Press, 2002).

4. Ahmed Alaidy, *Being Abbas el Abd*, trans. Humphrey Davies (Cairo: AUC Press, 2006).

5. Miral al-Tahawy, *The Tent*, trans. Anthony Calderbank (Cairo: AUC Press, 1998).

6. A collection edited by Margot Badran and Miriam Cooke presents the range of Arab women's writing: *Opening the Gates: An Anthology of Arab Feminist Writing* (Bloomington: University of Indiana Press, 2004).

7. Qassem Amin, *The Liberation of Women* and *The New Woman*, trans. Samiha Sidhom Peterson (Cairo: AUC Press, 2000).

8. Quotations from Leila Ahmed, *Women and Gender in Islam* (New Haven: Yale University Press, 1992), chapter 8.

9. Quotations from Shaarawi's autobiography, translated as *Harem Years* by Marilyn Booth (New York: Feminist Press, 1987).

10. Ahmed writes that Shaarawi's 'perspective was informed by a Western affiliation and a westernizing outlook and apparently by a valorization of Western ways as more advanced and more "civilized" than native ways' (*Women and Gender in Islam* , 1992).

11. Ihsan Abdel-Quddus, *I Am Free*, trans. Trevor Le Gassick (Cairo: General Egyptian Book Organisation, 1978).

12. Leila Baalbaki, *I Live*, French trans. by Michel Barbot as *Je vis* (Paris: Seuil, 1961).

13. Leila Baalbaki, 'A Spaceship of Tenderness to the Moon', trans. Denys Johnson-Davies, in *Modern Arabic Short Stories* (London: Heinemann, 1976), pp. 128–134.

14. As noted by Roger Allen in his survey of 'The Mature Arabic Novel outside Egypt' (in M. M. Badawi, ed. *Modern Arabic Literature*, Cambridge: Cambridge University Press, 1992), pp. 193–222.

15. Latifa al-Zayyat, *The Open Door*, trans. Marilyn Booth (Cairo: AUC Press, 2001). There is a well-known film version of this novel starring Faten Hamama (dir. Henri Barakat, 1964).

16. Both Nawal al-Saadawi's *Women at Point Zero* (London: Zed, 1983) and *The Hidden Face of Eve* (London: Zed, 1980) are translated by Sherif Hetata.

17. Quotations from Nawal al-Saadawi, *Memoirs of a Woman Doctor*, trans. Catherine Cobham (London: Saqi, 1988).

18. Quotations from Nawal al-Saadawi, *Memoirs from the Women's Prison,* trans. Marilyn Booth (London: Women's Press, 1986).

19. May Telmissany, *Dunyazad*, trans. Roger Allen (London: Saqi, 2000).

20. Stories collected in Alifa Rifaat, *Distant View of a Minaret*, trans. Denys Johnson-Davies (London: Heinemann, 1983).

21. Stories collected in Salwa Bakr, *The Wiles of Men*, trans. Denys Johnson-Davies (London: Quartet, 1992).

22. See Hourani (*A History of the Arab Peoples*, 2002), chapter 25.

23. Quotations from Miriam Cooke's *War's Other Voices: Women Writers on the Lebanese Civil War* (1996). Cooke calls this group the 'Beirut Decentrists'.

24. Hanan al-Shaykh, *The Story of Zahra*, trans. Peter Ford (London: Quartet, 1991).

25. Hanan al-Shaykh, *Women of Sand and Myrrh*, trans. Catherine Cobham (New York: Doubleday, 1992).

26. Hanah al-Shaykh, *Only in London*, trans. Catherine Cobham (London: Bloomsbury, 2002).

27. Ghada Samman, *Beirut Nightmares*, trans. Nancy Roberts (London: Quartet, 1997).

28. Stephan Guth's essay 'The Function of Sexual Passages in some Egyptian Novels of the 1980s' is a useful *tour d'horizon*, arguing that descriptions of sexuality are intended to 'widen the scope of reality' and what can be publicly discussed (in R. Allen, H. Kilpatrick and Ed de Moor (eds.), *Love and Sexuality in Modern Arabic Literature*, London: Saqi, 1995, pp. 123–130).

29. See the legal survey by the International Lesbian and Gay Association at www.ilga.org, which also indicates the social stigma involved.

30. Raouf Moussad writes on these issues in his 'Objectively Marginalised', *al-Ahram Weekly*, 6 July 2006 (online at: http://weekly.ahram.org. eg/2006/802/cu6.htm).

31. Brian Whitaker, *Unspeakable Love: Gay and Lesbian Life in the Middle East* (London: Saqi, 2006), quotations from chapter 7.

32. Frédéric Lagrange gives the historical background in his 'Male Homosexuality in Modern Arabic Literature', already cited in connection with the novels of Sonallah Ibrahim (see footnote 13 to the previous chapter).

33. Hoda Barakat, *The Tiller of Waters*, trans. Marilyn Booth (Cairo: AUC Press, 2001).

34. Hoda Barakat, *The Stone of Laughter*, trans. Sophie Bennett (Reading: Garnet, 1994).

35. Interview with Hoda Barakat in *Le Monde* (15 June 2007).

36. Idris Ali, *Dongola*, trans. Peter Theroux (Fayetteville: University of Arkansas Press, 1998) and Haggag Hassan Oddoul, *Nights of Musk*, trans. Anthony Calderbank (Cairo: AUC Press, 2005).

37. Ibrahim al-Koni, *The Bleeding of the Stone*, trans. May Jayyusi and Christopher Tingley (New York: Interlink, 2001).

Conclusion

1. Sabry Hafez describes this atmosphere in his 'The Novel, Politics and Islam', *New Left Review* 5, September–October 2000, pp. 117–141, which focuses on the withdrawal of the novel *A Banquet for Seaweed* by Syrian writer Haydar Haydar. Taha Hussein was forced to withdraw his book on pre-Islamic poetry – poetry written before the advent of Islam – in 1926 'because it suggested a critical method which, if applied to the texts of religion, might cast doubt on their authenticity, and ... it struck at the roots of the traditional structure of Arabic learning' (A. Hourani, *Arabic Thought in the Liberal Age*, Oxford: Oxford University Press, 1962).

2. See Khaled Dawoud's 'Control without bounds?' at http://weekly.ahram.org.eg/2002/593/eg6.htm. Naguib Surur (d. 1978) was recognized as a poet and playwright of genius by his peers from the 'generation of the 1960s'.

3. Quotations from P. Cachia, *An Overview of Modern Arabic Literature* (Edinburgh: Edinburgh University Press, 1990).

4. Paul Starkey, *Modern Arabic Literature* (Edinburgh: Edinburgh University Press, 2006).

5. Elias Khoury, *Gate of the Sun* (London: Vintage, 2006) and Alaa Al Aswany, *The Yacoubian Building*, trans. Humphrey Davies (New York: Harper, 2006). The novels have also been made into films: *The Yacoubian Building* (dir. Marwan Hamed, 2006), and *Gate of the Sun* (dir. Yousry Nasrallah, 2004).

6. See the wide-ranging interview with Khoury, 'Politics and Culture in Lebanon', on the Lebanese Center for Policy Studies Website (http://www.lcps-lebanon.org/pub/breview/br5/khourybr5.html).

7. Alaa Al Aswany, *Chicago* (Cairo: Dar el-Shurouq, 2007).

Further Reading

Most references are given in endnotes to the text. However, it may be useful to have the following standard or reference works listed in one place.

For listings of the works of individual Arab authors in English translation, see Salih J. Altoma, *Modern Arabic Literature in Translation* (London: Saqi, 2005). Other bibliographical or reference works include those edited by Paul Starkey and Julie Scott Meisami, *Encyclopedia of Arabic Literature* (London: Routledge, 1998, 2 vols.), which includes entries on classical Arabic literature as well as on modern, and by John J. Donohue and Leslie Tramontani, *Crosshatching in Global Culture: A Dictionary of Modern Arab Writers* (Beirut and Würzburg: Orient-Institut and Ergon Verlag, 2004, 2 vols.), which gives biographical or autobiographical entries for Arab authors and full bibliographies. A French reference book is Jamel-Eddin Bencheikh (ed.), *Dictionnaire de littératures arabe et maghrébine francophone* (Paris: Presses universitaires de France, 2000).

Useful anthologies of modern Arabic literature are given in endnotes to the text. In addition, there is *Modern Arabic Fiction: An*

Anthology (New York: Columbia University Press, 2005), edited by Salma Khadra Jayyusi, and, easier to handle, *The Anchor Book of Modern Arabic Fiction* (New York: Anchor, 2006), edited by Denys Johnson-Davies. A convenient general history is Albert Hourani, *A History of the Arab Peoples* (London: Faber & Faber, 2002), which may be supplemented by historical works by country and topic. Hourani's book includes an extensive bibliography, unfortunately not updated since 1991. A standard work on the earlier period is Hourani, *Arabic Thought in the Liberal Age* (Oxford: Oxford University Press, 1962). For Egypt, *The History of Modern Egypt* (Baltimore: Johns Hopkins, 1991) by P. J. Vatikiotis is especially useful. An essential reference work on all aspects of traditional and religious culture is *The Encyclopedia of Islam* (Leiden: Brill, 12 vols.). A monument of scholarship edited by authorities in the field, the *Encyclopedia* is now on its third edition, and articles from this and from the second edition can be consulted online.

General critical surveys of modern Arabic literature include those by Paul Starkey, *Modern Arabic Literature* (Edinburgh: Edinburgh University Press, 2006), Pierre Cachia, *An Overview of Modern Arabic Literature* (Edinburgh: Edinburgh University Press, 1990) and Roger Allen, *The Arabic Novel* (Syracuse: Syracuse University Press, 1995). There is also M. M. Badawi's *Short History of Modern Arabic Literature* (Oxford: Clarendon Press, 1995) and the same author's edited volume in the Cambridge History of Arabic Literature series, *Modern Arabic Literature* (Cambridge: Cambridge University Press, 1992). All these books contain bibliographies.

French publishers tend to be more active than English in the field of modern Arabic literature: it is worth keeping an eye on new French titles for those able to read the language.

On contemporary trends, the British literary magazine *Banipal* may be consulted, which features translated extracts. *Al-Ahram*

Weekly, published in Cairo by Al-Ahram, features material on contemporary Arabic literature and can be read online. Certain publishers, Saqi in Britain, the American University in Cairo Press in Egypt and New York, and various American university presses (for example Syracuse and Arkansas), publish translations of modern Arabic literature. Announcements can be consulted on the Internet. Web searches also turn up collections of Arabic literature in translation, especially poetry, hosted by various, usually academic, institutions.

Index

Page numbers in *italic* indicate an illustration.